Agents of Change

Proceedings of the Twenty-ninth Annual
Symposium of the Graduate Alumni and Faculty
of the Rutgers School of Communication,
Information and Library Studies, 12 April 1991

Agents of Change: Progress and Innovation in the Library/ Information Profession

Edited by Jana Varlejs

McFarland & Company, Inc., Publishers
Jefferson, North Carolina, and London

This is the tenth in a McFarland series of Rutgers SCILS symposia under the general editorship of Jana Varlejs. The first nine are *The Economics of Information* (1982), *The Right to Information* (1984), *Communication/Information/Libraries* (1985), *Freedom of Information and Youth* (1986), *Information Seeking* (1987), *Information and Aging* (1988), *Leadership in the Library/Information Profession* (1989), *Information Ethics* (1990), and *Information Literacy* (1991).

British Library Cataloguing-in-Publication data are available

Library of Congress Cataloguing-in-Publication Data

Agents of change : progress and innovation in the library/information
profession / edited by Jana Varlejs.
     p. cm.
    Includes bibliographical references.
    ISBN 0-89950-754-9 (sewn softcover : 55# alk. paper) ∞
    1. Information science — Congresses. 2. Organizational change —
Congresses. I. Varlejs, Jana.
Z665.A29 1992
020 — dc20   92-50322
                                                        CIP

Manufactured in the United States of America

McFarland & Company, Inc., Publishers
  Box 611, Jefferson, North Carolina 28640

1991 Honorary Alumni Award Citation

The annual symposium of the graduate alumni and faculty of the Rutgers School of Communication, Information and Library Studies is the occasion for adding the name of a distinguished graduate to the roll of individuals who have brought honor to the School through their achievements. The 1991 symposium departed somewhat from this custom by conferring honorary membership in the association upon Lowell Martin, the founding dean of the Rutgers Graduate School of Library Service. The citation presented to him on April 12 read as follows:

TRIBUTE TO LOWELL A. MARTIN

Whereas Lowell A. Martin is an innovator and change agent, as exemplified by his impact on the American Library Association's *Planning and Role Setting for Public Libraries,* and

Whereas for fifty years, his influence as consultant, educator, writer, and professional leader has pervaded the library profession's thinking about public library standards and services, and

Whereas he was instrumental in developing a plan for statewide library service which served New Jersey well for nearly twenty years, and which still is a model for library cooperation, and

Whereas Lowell A. Martin, as first dean of the Rutgers Graduate School of Library Service, set the new school on the high road toward excellence,

Therefore, be it resolved, that the Graduate Alumni of the Rutgers School of Communication, Information and Library Studies bestow upon Lowell A. Martin honorary membership in the Association, and

Be it further resolved, that this distinction be spread upon the minutes of this Association and be made known to the library community.

Acknowledgments

Thanks to Martha Hess, president of the Graduate Alumni of SCILS, and executive committee members Michele Maiullo and Barbara Sikora for their help with planning and logistics. Thanks to Scarecrow Press Vice President Norman Horrocks for his gracious acceptance of the award on behalf of Lowell Martin. Special appreciation is owed Betty Turock for contributing more than was called for to the proceedings, and for her skilled performance as moderator. We are particularly grateful to Mary Niles Maack for her bibliography on Lowell Martin, a project that she had undertaken independently, but fortunately was willing to contribute to this publication. Above all, we thank the speakers for their lively presentations.

Table of Contents

Preface:
Perspectives on Change Agentry

Jana Varlejs

We wanted the topic for the twenty-ninth annual symposium to reflect our desire to pay tribute to Lowell Martin, who was to receive honorary membership in the alumni association on this occasion. In reviewing his many achievements, we agreed that it was as a consultant that he had the greatest impact. That impact is most visible in the public library planning process which has evolved through the Public Library Association's sponsorship over the last decade. The notion of "role setting" can be traced directly to his analysis of library services in conjunction with the many studies of libraries which he conducted over the years (see Appendix B), and articulated most clearly in his Bowker lecture ("The Public Library: Middle-age Crisis or Old Age? *Library Journal,* January 1, 1983).

"Change agent" came to mind as an apt way to characterize someone who has had such a substantial influence on librarianship. We then began to think more generally about change in the field, and how it comes about: through individual leadership, through institutions, through technology. In speculating about the wellsprings of innovation, we realized that these resided both within the profession and also in the information industry that serves the library market. We also recognized our bias: our assumption was that change, on the whole, is positive and progressive, and therefore desirable. We were not so clear about what kinds of change we wanted to talk about, and as a result the symposium speakers covered a wide territory — from specific technical and managerial innovations, to emerging service priorities, to shifting philosophies of librarianship. In the end, however, it turned out that it was the *process* of change, rather than the agent of change that dominated the discussions. Even Betty Turock's introduction, which reviews the pertinent management literature, reveals a concern for the human dynamics that create a tug-of-war between stability and chaos.

With Lowell Martin's role of consultant as change agent in mind, we asked Mary Jo Lynch to share her thoughts on individuals she knew who play that role today. She added association executives to her list, because they often perform a similar change-agent role. Her paper provides useful insights into how these individuals operate and how they perceive their roles. For the most part, her informants seem to focus on facilitating change and helping their clients to solve their problems in a collaborative process. Unlike Lowell Martin, they usually do not try to move librarianship as a whole in a new direction.

In fact, only rarely can we attribute a major shift — in *how* things are done, or *what* things are done — to a single person. A prime exception, of course, is Melvil Dewey, as John Berry reminds us in his contribution to the symposium. More recently, Hugh Atkinson, Fred Kilgour, and Henriette Avram spring to mind — leaders who played crucial roles in the development of our now pervasive bibliographic networks. The look of modern library buildings owes much to Ralph Ellsworth, who is largely responsible for today's typically open, multipurpose layout. Our awareness of the importance of continuing education can be attributed to Betty Stone, who persists tenaciously in trying to institutionalize that function as a priority of national and international professional associations. Inequities suffered by women in librarianship were brought to the fore by Anita Schiller, Kathleen Heim, Leigh Estabrook, Pat Schuman, Kathleen Weibel, and others — it would be hard to pinpoint a single change agent in this case. Indeed, this movement, spearheaded by a group, is more illustrative of how change occurs in our profession than the earlier examples cited. Ideas that resonate find supporters who sometimes collaborate, sometimes stake out their own ancillary campaigns. Leadership becomes diffuse, and is then submerged in a bandwagon, as more and more people sign on. John Berry describes this phenomenon at length in his paper.

Individuals and groups are not the only change agents. Often it seems that a new technology, by its mere appearance on the scene, spurs innovation. Sometimes an institution — the Baltimore County Public Library, for example — models new approaches. As BCPL director Charlie Robinson points out in his paper, he as administrator is pushed and pulled by a multitude of intra- and extra-institutional forces, and cannot by himself claim to be the "change agent."

Other kinds of institutions that might play the role of change agent in the profession include the press, library education, state library agencies, organizations such as the Research Libraries Group, professional associations, the National Commission on Libraries and Information Science, the Office of Educational Research and Improvement of the Department of Education (through which federal monies are channeled to libraries), the Council on Library Resources, and so on. All of these institutions share a common mission—the improvement of library and information services—and are therefore potential change agents. The symposium did not attempt to deal with the question of the relative effectiveness of these various bodies, although John Berry touched on some. The interaction of these organizations in the diffusion of innovation would make for a fascinating study. Meanwhile, we can turn to Verna Pungitore's instructive *Study of the Development and Diffusion of the Public Library Association's Planning and Evaluation Manuals* (Indiana University, 1989), which shows the importance of association and state agency roles in stimulating change.

Most of us think first of technology when we contemplate recent changes in our field and ponder what drives these changes. There is no question that the computer has revolutionized the library/information field, but one can raise lots of questions about the dynamics involved in introducing automated systems and electronic information services. As Betty Eddison points out in her account of the genesis of Inmagic, the impulse to make things work better needs to be linked to a professional analysis of the problem, and then to the ideas, tools, and skills required to solve the problem. Successful innovation demands a synergy of our professional knowledge and vision with outside technical expertise. When the synergy is out of balance, as happened in the case of CLSI, according to John Berry, costly mistakes are made.

The relationship between librarians and the vendors and consultants who serve the library market is a fascinating area to explore further. Betty Eddison is not the only success story of a librarian with a good idea crossing over into information industry entrepreneurship. For example, there is Joe Ward, who created *Microcomputer Index* and then went on to run a software company (*Library Journal,* September 15, 1985). Art Brody, the chairman of Brodart, was never a librarian, but exemplifies the entrepreneur who has a synergistic relationship with librarians. As did Betty Eddison, he fell into library product development by accident (*Library Journal,* December 1989). He attributes his success to listening to librarians, acting on their ideas, and seizing opportunities. The products and services he has developed, from clear book covers to fully processed opening day collections, to *The Elementary School Library Collection,* to the McNaughton plan — all have helped to change how librarians do things in a productive way.

Eugene Garfield is another entrepreneur of note. His creation of citation indexes in the sciences has spawned not only indispensable reference tools, but also a whole body of research based on the indexes. The resulting insights into scholarly communication, the importance of journals to their discipline, the emergence of new fields, and so on, have both theoretical and practical value for the profession.

The symposium papers, together with the closing discussion session, touch on many aspects of change agentry and, as usual, raise more questions than they answer. Advances in the practice of librarianship depend upon a complex mix of individual leadership and professional bandwagons, planning and accident, research and serendipity, fresh inspiration and evolving tradition. While it may look as though major change is driven largely by new technology or shifting economic climates — environments impinging on the profession from without — it is always the human agent who determines whether opportunities are seized or lost.

Introduction:
Creating Organizations
Where Change Flourishes

Betty J. Turock

Libraries are not unlike other organizations in their need to innovate. The magnitude of change impacting the economy has left the country reeling. Since the market crash of 1987 from which the economy never fully recovered to the current recession, we have heard more and more of the Zero Sum Society, popularized by Lester Thurow in his two books *The Zero-Sum Society* and *The Zero-Sum Solution*.[1] There, finances are limited and more money for one program at the national, state, or local level means less money for another, so that the overall effect is zero growth in spending.

We know he is on to something because during the 1980's, more than four thousand of our largest corporations went through massive restructuring. A survey of the American Management Association's council members demonstrated that more than one-third of their organizations had downsized in 1989 and over 20 percent did so in 1990.[2] It is clear that the conditions giving rise to this abrupt, headlong fall from grace — foreign competition; deregulation; depressed world markets in oil and agriculture; an overvalued, then devalued dollar — continue to precipitate change.

Besides economic fluctuations we are also operating in an environment where the structure of the organization, the organization of work, the increasing diversity of the workforce, and the massive introduction of technology bound together by the convergence of the computer and video, have altered organizational culture beyond recognition.

At conferences like this, for over a decade we have heard that we are operating libraries in a world that is subject to change without notice, that the only thing we can be sure of is change. In fact, during this time period, the only immutable has been the emphasis on change and its resulting transformations. We have learned of the magnitude of these transformations and the magnitude of the response that is required to meet them. We are convinced that we must live within innovative organizations to thrive or at least to survive and we search valiantly for the keys to becoming what Rosabeth Moss Kanter, one of today's major management theorists, has called a change master—a person adept at the art of anticipating the need for, and of leading, productive change.[3]

We look for guides to help us create organizations where innovation flourishes. But the messages we receive about how to reach this exalted state are mixed and confusing. Kanter advises that we must learn a new set of skills. To create more flexible, integrated, innovation-stimulating environments, we need power skills—the ability to persuade others to invest information, support, and resources in new initiatives; the ability to manage the problems associated with the greater use of teams and employee participation; and the understanding of how change is designed and constructed in an organization. We must be able to create cultures of pride, climates of success.[4]

Another management theorist of the day, Tom Peters, author of the best selling *In Search of Excellence* describes the necessity for us to master a new way of structuring work.[5] The conventional wisdom calls for an organizational chart that clearly delineates one managerial fiefdom from another, one position within the fiefdom from another, and job descriptions that detail responsibilities exactly. Lines of authority are precisely drawn and tasks are specific.

But Peters makes it clear that the real world of organizations no longer has order as a hallmark. He agrees with Kanter that a clearly defined job in a simple structure barely exists in an innovating, change-driven organization. Today, assignments are ambiguous, functions are vaguely defined, authority is indeterminate, and resources uncertain. The tenet that creativity derives from structure has been laid to rest, replaced by the more daunting dictum that creativity arises from shared participation in inventing order where there is none.

To survive, Peters reasons that managers must learn to thrive on chaos.[6] Both Peters and Kanter reinforce the fact that where innovation flourishes, organizations are participative and the workforce at every level is involved in tackling and solving problems. Once solely the

6 Agents of Change

job of top managers who worked secretly to hide the challenges their organizations confronted, now it is understood that talent is widely dispersed and greater participation can turn up more adaptive answers.

The organization of work is no longer along the lines of the hierarchical pyramid, but it is as Peter Drucker has called it, "free form."[7] Teams, put together on the basis of expertise to solve the problem posed, provide the new work structure. In this matrix management environment there is an overlay of flexibility, problem-solving task forces, joint planning ventures, and information-sharing assemblies. Incentives for initiative abound. Jobs are not clearly drawn; they are nonroutine and change oriented. Territorial imperatives are diminished and teams produce intersections among a number of organizational units. Any progress or action requires cooperation across lines of authority, since the resulting innovation effects changes that cross organizational lines as well.

Autonomy is the bulwark of this initiative driven environment. To move ahead, those who would innovate do not need to return at each turn for higher level approval. Still, cooperation is rewarded and it is understood that innovation requires floating new boundaries instead of honoring old ones. As Kanter sums it, "To produce innovation, more complexity is essential; more relationships, more sources, more angles on problems, more ways to pull in human and material resources, more freedom to walk around and across the organization."[8] The result we seek is a self-enforcing upward cycle — performance stimulating pride stimulation performance.

Paul Hershey and Kenneth Blanchard invoke Kurt Lewin's force field analysis to help us achieve that end.[9] Once discrepancies are established between what is actually happening and the innovation that is desired, they are analyzed using the force field. The questions we seek to answer are, "What is driving innovation and what is restraining it?" If this is not done, these management consultants advise, we can begin implementing a change strategy and be blown out of the water without knowing why.

For all five, Kanter, Peters, Drucker, Hershey and Blanchard, the workers most concerned with the welfare of the organization are not the ones who claim that nothing needs to be improved. They are the ones who proclaim organizational faults at every opportunity while, at the same time, they try to rectify them.

We face the twenty-first century when in our nation cultural diversity will be more than just a buzz word. In that milieu empowerment is a prerequisite to change. It is not enough to build a more diverse workforce, we must empower that workforce by giving its members tasks that require the use of judgment to resolve problems that are central to the existence of the organization. Only in raising their visibility and credibility can workers from diverse cultures gain the power needed to become significant players in innovation and change.

But to empower the workforce, we need to discover what makes power more widely distributed in some organizations than in others. What conditions help, what power tools (as Kanter has termed them) — information (data, technical knowledge, political intelligence, expertise); resources (funds, materials, space, time); and support (endorsement, backing, approval, legitimacy) — circulate so that they can be grabbed and used by anyone who needs them?[10]

Innovation leads to a disruption in existing activities and a redirection of the organization's energies to make the switch to new strategies, markets, work distribution, and technologies; and to provide enhanced products and service. Power tools must be available to all those involved in change and this inherently creates resistance. Change masters must be equipped to counteract its downdrafts.

The psychologist and library educator, Sara Fine, writes convincingly that the real key to managing change is not to begin with the change itself, but with the psychology of human behavior and with attention to what change will look like and feel like to those whom it affects.[11] She uses the Gulf War as an example to point out the realities of resistance. During the conflict, she reminds us, we were supplied with sometimes overwhelming amounts of information about the advanced weapons our troops were taking into combat, weapons made possible through advanced technology. But many of them had not been tested under fire and none of the troops depending on their accuracy, dependability, and speed knew if they would perform as expected.

We frequently hear that library technology does not perform as expected either, but, just as in the Gulf War, the success of innovations depends on more than technological competency. Fine calls the gap between what machines can do and what people who use them can do, the human factor, and denotes that gap one of the major reasons for the success or failure of innovations. Library managers are well acquainted with the human factor. It is frequently disguised as disappointment in expensive new computer systems. But is it the technology alone that disappoints or is it, at least in large part, lack of understanding of the human factor?

To create an organization where change flourishes we must attend to the basic principle that humans, like other living organisms, attempt to maintain homeostasis — a balance. When endangered by the effects of change, they will engage in a mighty effort to regain equilibrium. Fine admonishes us to remember that change is governed by the potential, limits, and demands of human nature. These demands — for order, structure, dependability, and predictability, on one hand, and excitement, stimulation, and variety, on the other hand — are on a collision course during change, if managers do not take the human need for equilibrium into account.

In the dynamic society surrounding today's libraries, the question of whether change, with its concomitant resistance, will occur is no longer relevant. Instead the issues become: How do we as library managers and leaders cope with the inevitable barrage of changes that confront us and still keep our organizations viable? How do we create the innovation needed for survival? How do we retain equilibrium as we are forced to move ahead at unprecedented speed?

For the future, research has a part in making us able to play the role of change masters. John Seely Brown makes a crucial connection for us between research and practice when he says, "As organizations try to keep pace with rapid changes and cope with increasingly unstable environments, research must design the new technological and organizational architectures that make possible a continuously innovating organization."[12] Put another way, research must reinvent innovation. Innovation surrounds us; we must look at it closely and learn from it. We must find out how organizations accept and reject innovations to illuminate the cultural features of organizations that lead to change. Research must also point the way to move from the building blocks of innovation to the institutionalization of change by joining micro-innovations to macro-innovations that strategically reorient the whole organization.

So we are given organizations where change is part of the everyday work life. Run by change masters, their workforce is diverse and empowered and expected to invent, develop, or plan something that leads to organizational advancement. This cultural image of success is driven by research that leads the way to moving from small and large organizational changes to the institutionalization of innovation. To help us take that leap, in the following papers, four librarians who by anyone's standards would be called change masters let us know whether they agree with the profile of change that has been set forth by the current management gurus.

References

1. Lester C. Thurow, *The Zero-Sum Society* (New York: Basic Books, 1980) and *The Zero-Sum Solution* (New York: Simon and Schuster, 1985).

2. Ronald D. Elliott, "The Challenge of Managing Change," *Personnel World* (March 1990):40.

3. Rosabeth Moss Kanter, *The Change Masters: Innovation and Entrepreneurship in the American Corporation* (New York: Simon and Schuster, 1983), 13.

4. Kanter, *Change Masters*, 129.

5. Thomas J. Peters and Robert H. Waterman, Jr., *In Search of Excellence: Lessons from America's Best-Run Companies* (New York: Harper & Row, 1982).

6. Tom Peters, *Thriving on Chaos* (New York: Knopf; distributed by Random House, 1987).

7. Peter Drucker, *Technology, Management and Society* (New York: Harper & Row, 1970), 113.

8. Kanter, *Change Masters,* 148.

9. Paul Hershey and Kenneth Blanchard, *Management of Organizational Behavior* (Englewood Cliffs, NJ: Prentice-Hall, 1988), 135–37.

10. Rosabeth Moss Kanter, *Men and Women of the Corporation* (New York: Basic Books, 1977), chapter 7.

11. Sara Fine, "Change and Resistance," *The Bottom Line* 5 (Spring 1991):18–23.

12. John Seely Brown, "Research that Reinvents the Corporation," *Harvard Business Review* 69 (January–February 1991):102–11.

The Individual as Change Agent: Consultants and Association Executives as Provocateurs and Persuaders

Mary Jo Lynch

It is a great pleasure to be back at Rutgers, to be part of a program on change—a topic that is so central to our personal and professional lives. Usually when people ask me to speak, it is because of something I've done or written that indicates that I have special knowledge of the topic. That isn't true in this case, at least not on the surface. I've never done research on change and I have never written about it. I'm not a consultant and, though I am an association executive, my own role in fostering change has not been one to attract much attention.

To tell the truth, I don't really like change very much. At least not change that disturbs my own life. But there certainly is no way of avoiding it. That was brought home to me with special force recently while visiting a friend in California. I had gone to San Diego in March for the PLA's national conference and spent the weekend with the woman who had been my best friend from age seven to seventeen. We haven't seen much of each other in the last twenty years and had a lot of catching up to do. Those years had been good to Liz. She has a successful husband who built shopping centers all over the San Diego area, a beautiful home, three lovely children now with degrees from prestigious colleges. But, things have not always been smooth. About ten years ago when her husband had several deals going at once and all of the kids were coming and going at a rapid pace, Liz went to a family psychologist for help in coping. After listening for a while, he asked Liz "What do you really want?" She replied, "for just two weeks,

I'd like nothing to change." "Oh," he said, "what you want is to be dead." That's not what she wanted, not what any of us want. Still, change is disturbing.

When Jana asked me to speak today my first impulse was to think about someone else to suggest. Then I realized that I knew a lot of people who do consulting or bring about change as association executives and that I would enjoy interviewing them about change. Furthermore, I admired the other people Jana proposed for the panel and would enjoy sharing the program with them. Also, I couldn't say no to my alma mater. So I said yes.

Thoughts on Lowell Martin

Before I tell you what I learned in those interviews, I'd like to say a few words about Lowell Martin. When I started doctoral work at Rutgers in 1973, it was indirectly because of Lowell Martin. Indirectly, because Martin had been a strong influence on Terry Crowley whose unobtrusive testing of reference service was the first research to challenge the assumption that reference service was always accurate and the first in our field to use what Eugene Webb had termed "unobtrusive measures." Crowley first studied reference service accuracy while a student at Rutgers working for Lowell Martin in a Pennsylvania survey. Later, he discovered unobtrusive measures and used them in his doctoral dissertation. Shortly thereafter, Thomas Childers built on Crowley's work in another Rutgers dissertation.

When I decided to do a doctorate, I wanted a program that would help me do meaningful research on reference service. The Crowley and Childers studies done at Rutgers were what attracted me here originally. I never met Lowell Martin in my student days but I asked Tom Childers recently what he was like as a teacher. Tom praised Lowell Martin highly, especially for his scholarship, originality, and reconceptualization of the public library.

Terry Crowley praised him for similar reasons and went on to speak of Lowell's inspirational leadership of the team that produced *Library Response to Urban Change,* the landmark study of the Chicago Public Library published by ALA in 1969. One of the consultants to that project, Virginia Mathews, then of the National Book Committee, was in my office at ALA shortly after I agreed to speak here today. I asked her what she remembered most about Lowell Martin and she spoke in glowing terms about his marvelous skill in asking questions that made people think.

It was because of his own thinking about the public library that I did meet Lowell Martin several years after I left Rutgers. He sat next to me at the dinner that kicked off a workshop on the draft manuscript of *A Planning Process for Public Libraries*. That manuscript, published by ALA in 1980, was produced and tested with the support of a federal grant, the first proposal for which was drafted here at Rutgers by PLA leaders with the help of Professors Ralph Blasingame and Ernest De Prospo. It wasn't funded right away but when it *was* funded I was on staff at ALA and responsible for coordinating the project. Using material originally developed in connection with a consulting project at Baltimore County Public Library, Gene Palmour and his colleagues at King Research described how public librarians could tailor their service to the circumstances and needs of a particular community. After the manuscript had been drafted and tested, we convened a group of public librarians at a resort outside Chicago to work through it in an "imaginary dry run" of the process. Lowell Martin was asked to speak at the first dinner because the idea of planning library service based on local needs and conditions was one of the ideas he championed. He gave an inspirational talk that night but warned us that this kind of planning would not become popular right away. It is for the leaders, he told us, not the "laggards."

As many of you know, that first planning process volume has now been revised and, again, Lowell Martin and other Rutgers people were involved. Rutgers Ph.D. Charles McClure led the five-person study team that produced *Planning and Role Setting for Public Libraries* (ALA, 1987). I was also on the team, as was Douglas Zweizig who did his master's at Rutgers. One of the documents we pondered and argued over a lot was Lowell Martin's 1982 Bowker Memorial lecture "The Public Library: Middle-age Crisis or Old Age?" (*Library Journal* [January 1983]:17–22).

The eight possible roles for public libraries described in *Planning and Role Setting* were based very directly on Martin's suggestions in that Bowker lecture. The idea of choosing roles and building a service program around that choice may not be sweeping the country but it is spreading. More and more when public librarians describe what they are doing or not doing, they mention one or more of those roles. Public library planning based on roles is a change that Lowell Martin definitely influenced. I have the sense that there is a lot more to be known about his influence on changes in our field and I hope someone explores that topic in more detail eventually.

Interviews about Change

What I did for this speech was to ask five questions of twelve people who are friends and/or professional colleagues. They either do consulting or are executives in library associations. In my view, all are change agents. The questions were as follows:

- Do you think of yourself as someone who initiates or instigates change? If not, why not?
- If yes, have you *always* thought of yourself that way?
- Do you think your clients see you that way?
- Do you use any specific techniques, consciously or instinctively?
- Based on your own experience, what advice would you give others seeking to initiate or instigate change?

The interviewees were a mix of library school faculty who do consulting on the side, independent consultants who do it for a living, and library association executives. Both men and women were interviewed. They live in all parts of the country. None of the interviewees is a building consultant and only one is primarily an automation consultant. Most of the people I interviewed are not on any list now, but if someone developed a list of library planning or management or organizational consultants, these people would probably be included.

I'm not going to identify them by name in what follows. Not because anyone asked me to keep their remarks confidential, but because I think it will be more useful, in the brief time we have today, to focus on some general ideas and not be distracted by specific personalities and projects. I will not identify the sex of my sources in these remarks either. Instead I will adopt the alternate paragraph rule, i.e., the third person, personal pronoun will stay the same for a whole paragraph and will alternate throughout the paper, starting with "she" in deference to the high percentage of women in our field.

Perceptions of Self

My first question to them all was "Do you think of yourself as someone who initiates or instigates change?" As might be expected, given why I chose them, all answered "yes." But yes to the concept of being associated in a positive way with change, not necessarily with "initiating" or "instigating." Several of those I interviewed might be a little uncomfortable with the words in the title of this speech "provocateurs" and "persuaders." They saw themselves as helping to make change happen, but cautioned me that what they did was collaborative with their clients or members. One told me "It's their work. I listen to them, go away and do stuff with their ideas (organize, shape, fill in gaps), bring it back to them and start the cycle again." Another said "It's important to remember that a consultancy is not for the consultant, it's for the client."

That was not everyone's view, however. One interviewee told me "I've always looked for ways to make things better and I don't do consulting unless it allows me to effect change." He saw consulting as a blend of two motivations. "The client has a need to solve problems; I have a need to effect change." Another told me he sees consulting as an opportunity to move forward with his own applied research agenda. He only accepts consulting assignments that will provide such an opportunity. I have a little trouble with that because I believe there are important differences between consulting and research, but that's a topic for another day.

Only one of the interviewees liked change for its own sake. All the others saw change as a way to improve things or as a way to solve problems. Even the person who confessed to loving the challenge and excitement of change for its own sake was well aware that most people have a different view and that she needed to introduce change with care as well as enthusiasm. Another association executive saw change as identical with good management. When asked "What if no change is needed?" she replied "It always is. Something is always wrong or the outside environment has changed and you need to do the same."

When asked "Have you always thought of yourself that way?," (i.e., as someone promoting change) several told me they had been interested in change ever since they became aware of the concept. One mentioned that even as a child he had always wanted to improve things. Another observed that his fondness for change may have been a reaction to parents who always rejected it.

Relationship with Clients

When I asked the consultants how their clients perceived them, they didn't have a lot to say about client perception but they did talk a lot about how they select clients (or reject as the case may be). Everyone spoke of the importance of a good "match" between client and consultant both in terms of goals for the consultancy and in terms of personal chemistry. "Match" was the exact word used in most cases.

Several said they would not accept an assignment if they did not agree with the goals of the client. One spoke about the initial contacts between potential client and consultant as being like a courtship. Before a long term commitment is made there may be numerous discussions through which the two parties try to find out if they want to go forward together. On interviewee spoke of the need to set up a consultancy in stages so that it can be broken off if things are not going well.

One described three different relationships to change that may confront a consultant. A consultant can be asked to help a client prepare for change, cope with change, or fight change. The consultant who described this trinity told me she was not interested in the third type of assignment — fighting change is counterproductive and uninteresting. She much prefers the first type of assignment — helping clients prepare for change — but will accept the second if she agrees with where the client wants to go.

My one interviewee who is an automation consultant hesitated in answering that question about client perception and digressed for a minute to talk about a different trinity — the three stages of technological change: substitution, extension, and innovation. First you use technology to do what you've been doing, only better. Then you do additional things, finally you do very different things. This consultant observed that he and his firm are often hired to do stage one or maybe stage two because most librarians don't realize that stage three is possible or desirable. He much prefers assignments where clients are ready for stage three.

The association executives had a different perspective on the relationship with clients, in this case, members. For these people, for us because I am one of them, there is the constant tension between the need to exert leadership with member groups and the need to simply take orders. Library associations are not unique in this; it seems to be inherent in the nature of nonprofit, voluntary associations. Because there is constant turnover in the leadership and membership of such groups and the subgroups that arise within them, the executives that staff non-profit, voluntary associations must be adept at adapting and have a high tolerance for ambiguity. The world outside the association is changing constantly so an association must change its own operations and help its members to change theirs. Association executives are usually hired because they have good ideas and know how to get things done. Some members want those skills used to foster change — but some don't. And the cast of characters itself is constantly changing. Therein lies the challenge to association executives.

Techniques

When I asked the interviewees if they used any specific techniques, the same ideas kept coming up from interview to interview. Everyone told me right away something to the effect that "I listen a lot" and most mentioned the importance of getting people involved so that they can easily "buy into" something new. One talked about doing this by creating occasions when groups of those who will be affected can talk about plans for change and be involved in shaping them. The automation consultant was especially emphatic on this point. "Automation is a process," he said, "not a decision. It involves everyone in the library and my job is to 'empower' them to use the system. Getting people to work in teams across departmental and hierarchical categories is essential."

Another consultant described "assignments" he had asked the clients' staff to do that would expose them to reasons why change was needed. One association executive emphasized that people will certainly resent change if they perceive it as something done *to* them. Instead, you want people to welcome the change as something they do because they believe in it.

An independent consultant told me she helps clients see their situation in a new way (i.e., build a new conceptual framework) by using scenario building, worst case planning, nominal group technique. That same consultant spoke of the importance of getting language straight when working with organizations. She often focuses on vocabulary in order to clarify issues.

Several spoke of the need to act as coach and or cheerleader to clients who know what to do but need an outside force to help them do it, to give them confidence. He spoke of the importance of understanding the client organization and finding the people within it who have a vision but need help in translating it into action.

That conversation took place on March 28, the same day that I read a piece by Peter Drucker in the *Wall Street Journal* on "Don't Change Corporate Culture — Use It!" Drucker begins by saying:

> Changing the corporate culture has become the latest management fad. Every business magazine carries articles about it. And not a week goes by without my being asked to run a seminar on the subject.

He went on to say that change was certainly needed, but disagreed that it was always the culture that must go. Then he gave examples of effective change in organizations and pointed out that:

In every single case these results were achieved not by doing
something different but by systematically doing something
everyone had known all along should be done, had in the
policy manuals, and had been preaching—but only the few
exceptions had been practicing.

My interviewee referred to the Drucker piece which he had also read
that day and reported that it made sense in his experience.

Another article in the *Wall Street Journal*, this time on March 4,
supports ideas I heard in the interviews. The article was headed "Some
Manage; Some Muse; Some Do Both" and it was about philosophy ma-
jors finding a respected place in the worlds of consulting and finance.
The article talked about Edwin Hartman, with a degree in ancient
philosophy from Princeton, who "used the early Socratic dialogues to
help clients. By astute questioning of clients, he led them to their own
conclusions."

Later the article talks about Jay Harker of the Mercantile Bank
of St. Louis who has a Ph.D. in philosophy from the University of Illinois. Harker says his studies of Bertrand Russell's logic "help him
break office dilemmas into 'essential elements.' By isolating relevant information and throwing out the fluff, he simplified the bank's convo-
luted career paths and labyrinthine training program. He is careful,
however, to stop short of making customers prove they exist."

None of my interviewees had philosophy degrees, but several mentioned those techniques—using questions to help a client think through
a problem and breaking a problem into manageable chunks.

Advice

My final question was to ask what advice the interviewee would
give to others seeking to foster change. Actually, they all gave advice
throughout the interview and, as before, many told me the same things.
The most basic advice was that people don't change unless they want
to and most people resist change—at least at first. It has something to
do with the second law of thermodynamics.

Speaking more specifically of the work of a consultant, several
mentioned the importance of specializing in one type of assignment
and not taking on challenges in areas you are unfamiliar with. Once
you have the assignment, it is essential to be:

- absolutely honest with the client;
- firm about what you know to be right;

- flexible when possible;
- very careful what you say in public.

That last admonition is very important. Several mentioned it and one interviewee told me stories about otherwise successful consultancies he knew about that were seriously damaged in the end because the consultant criticized the client in front of the board to which the client reported. Being honest with the client is one thing; exposing the client's shortcomings is another.

Several spoke about the value of various kinds of training. Two mentioned the National Training Laboratory in Group Development at Bethel, Maine which developed the idea of a change agent and has done extensive work in identifying the skills needed. One had been through training for "mediators," people who specialize in helping others settle differences without litigation. Several recommended Myers-Briggs training, which helps one gain an appreciation of different character and temperament types. And one mentioned a similar but more powerful assessment tool, the "Birkman Method" which she used for team building. One had been through the consultant training provided by the Association of Research Libraries, which focuses on the logical steps in problem solving.

One interviewee highly recommended training in Neuro-Linguistic Programming (NLP). I had only a vague sense of what that might be so I looked into it a bit. NLP is not another programming language. As described on a brochure from the National Association of Neuro-Linguistic Programming, NLP is

> the study of subjective experience. NLP utilizes specific precise skills of communication, observation and conceptualization to understand the structure and functioning of an individual's unique personal reality. Such understanding can then be used to assist individuals and systems in a respectful manner, to reach desired outcomes, whether within themselves or in relationships with others. NLP has also developed procedures, called modeling, for identifying patterns of excellence in an individual and of transferring these resources to another person who may wish to acquire them. Modeling and the creative use of the understanding of the mind's workings have also allowed NLP to develop many efficient patterns for behavioral and emotional change which are applicable in many fields.

One of the basic ideas of NLP is that people are either visual ("I *see* what you mean") or auditory ("I *hear* you saying X") or kinesthetic

("I *feel* you are trying to tell me Y"). People can communicate much more effectively if they use the appropriate language systems. NLP is much more complicated than that and I'll stop now before I get in too deep.

I'd like to close by talking about what seemed to me the best advice to consultants, or association executives, or anyone wanting to see change happen in an organization: Rosabeth Moss Kanter. Dr. Kanter, now editor of the *Harvard Business Review*, wrote a very impressive monograph called *The Change Masters: Innovation and Entrepreneurship in the American Corporation* (Simon and Schuster, 1983). The essential ideas were embodied in a video produced later by Encyclopaedia Britannica also called *Change Masters*.

That video, which one of my interviewees watches at least once a month, begins with a comparison of today's business environment to the croquet game in Alice in Wonderland where the mallets are the long necks of tropical birds that constantly twist and turn, the balls are hedgehogs that periodically get up and walk away, and the wickets are picture cards — king, queen, jack, that are frequently moved around to different places on the playing field. The birds and the hedgehogs and the picture cards are all moving around on the screen as Kanter talks about the changes affecting corporations today. One could easily alter the text to describe the world of communication, information, and library studies. At least that's how it seems to me.

Then, Kanter describes the seven key characteristics of successful change masters and illustrates each with entertaining anecdotes. Change masters are:

1. Tuned in to the environment, to the world outside their own field;
2. Kaleidoscopic thinkers (i.e., able to relate seemingly disparate ideas);
3. Able to communicate a clear vision (e.g., I have a dream);
4. Adept at building coalitions (there are so many ways to defeat change, you need to work hard to get everyone on your side);
5. Able to work through teams;
6. Persistent;
7. Know how to make everyone a hero.

I looked at that video again last week and heard echoes of what I had heard in the interviews. Then I went back to the book and remembered why this had impressed me so much in the first place. The ideas in the book made sense and the illustrative anecdotes were impressive. But there is a lot of writing like this, what might be called "self help" literature for business. It always seems to be an explication of one individual's good ideas. I always wonder if the ideas are generalizable. What convinced me in *Change Masters* was the appendix where Kanter describes her research. The work that led to *Change Masters* took place over a period of five years, involved six focused studies on questions related to innovation, change, and corporate responsiveness to new environmental demands. It involved content analysis, structured observation, in depth interviews. In the appendix, Kanter describes what she did and the means she took to ensure the reliability and validity of her findings.

I'm grateful to the organizers of this event for the opportunity to get reacquainted with Rosabeth Moss Kanter and to talk about change with people I believe are effective change agents. Now I'm eager to hear what others have to say.

The Entrepreneur as Change Agent: Innovation Through Product and Service Genesis

Elizabeth Bole Eddison

Having sat and looked at the sign, which is now behind me, this being Cook College, I have decided that probably the most appropriate way to describe what I'm going to be talking about is in culinary terms. I think what you're going to get from me more than from any of the other speakers is something similar to a possibly complicated and elaborate goulash, but let us see where we go.

A lot of change happens by accident. It wasn't ever intended or carefully planned. I think any one of you will recognize that in your own lives. It certainly has happened in my life; it's why I'm here, in fact.

International Living

My husband had his doctorate in economic development. After he earned his degree, we started moving around the world, living in third world countries. We were very, very lucky. We spent some fourteen years in Burma, India, Pakistan, Bolivia and Colombia plus Puerto Rico (which isn't a foreign country but is a different culture).

You learn about change when you move every year or two or three from one country to another, from one language to another, from one national religion to another, from one culture to another. You learn to be very fast on your feet. You learn about change if you're moving with a family. You have two children, aged two and three, with whom you've struggled across the Atlantic in propeller planes. You were clutching more teddy bears and everything else you could possibly think of because you knew that the sea freight (i.e., most of your possessions) wasn't going to get there for three months anyway, and you had to get the family up and running in a new community as soon as you arrived. You learned a lot of skills.

This kind of life went on for some time. The last overseas assignment was in Bogota, Colombia. By then I had become something of an expert on international schools because one of my roles all the time we lived overseas was to do whatever I could to make the international school in that area one which would educate our children well.

One of the things that you saw a lot in Bogota was a great many Colombians wanting their children to come to college in the United States. It's close enough and there are strong commercial interests between the two countries. (This was twenty years ago, before the newer industries!) They wanted very much to make sure that they had well educated children so that the children could pass entrance exams to come here to school. The parents, therefore, brought a number of young American teachers to Colombia. Our youngest was in the second grade at the Colegio Nueva Granada, the binational school in Bogota. It had Colombians and U.S. students in it.

I arrived in Bogota thinking I had done my great public works. I was going to take a vacation. After about six weeks of settling in, life got boring. I had met the librarian at the school and I remembered that she had said that she didn't have time to order books, that she was so busy running the library and she didn't have any help. I went to her, told her how much I loved ordering books and offered to help her in that way. "Oh no," she said. "I want to order the books, but I'll tell you what we need." I said, "What's that?" She said, "What we need is to have subject access in our high school library." I said, "What?" She said, "Yes. We don't have any." I said, "Well how does anybody find anything?" She said, "Well, they use the Dewey Decimal index." I said, "Oh." Then I said, "Okay." There are times when people have wondered about my sanity.

I spent the next year and a half in one of the coldest rooms I have ever been in, assigning Sears subject headings to some seven thousand nonfiction books, 10–12 percent of which were in Spanish. If you have never catalogued a Spanish nonfiction book, you have missed an experience. The title may be the Spanish equivalent of "Oh My Soul." The table of contents will be the last page in the book. You have to be able to read enough Spanish to know that "Oh, My Soul," after you look at the table of contents and scan the introduction, is really describing the political situation in Argentina in 1933. It made an interesting and educational year and a half.

The bright young new educators had seen me wandering around the school in Bogota and they would ask me where I had gotten my education degree. I would respond that I didn't have one. Oh. Much dismay on their part, because here I was, after all, doing important things in the library. Well, where did I earn my library degree? The same response: I don't have one.

Professional Training

We went from Bogota to Cambridge, Massachusetts. By the time we got to Cambridge I had decided I needed a union card. That is, I needed some more initials after my name. Harvard was still not taking any part-time graduate students, otherwise I might have not gone into the library profession. (I might have gone into the education policy profession instead). But Simmons was offering a chance to earn a degree in library science on a part-time basis. I wasn't about to be a full-time graduate student with an eight year old in the middle of third grade.

I was a part-time graduate student when I first began as a change agent, first time around in the library world. This is how it happened.

By the time it was my turn to register one term, I found that the systems analysis course that Dick Palmer was teaching, and which I wanted to take, was full. The Registrar pointed out to me that I could take literature of the humanities, but I told the Registrar that I did not think they were comparable.

I was furious. I went racing upstairs to Dick Palmer, who was my advisor, and said, okay, what am I going to do now? And he looked at me and he asked me why didn't I do an independent research project? I told him that I couldn't because the deadlines were all past for submitting proposals and so forth. He said, never mind, he would take care of that.

Limited Library Service
for Spanish-Speaking Americans

My independent research project was a study of how Spanish language materials were handled in public libraries in communities which could be identified as having Spanish language populations. Getting the list of communities was the hardest part of the project because there was no single list. I had to compile one out of a number of pieces of other lists.

The questionnaire went out and got a phenomenal response. I never understood why. Eighty percent or more of them came back with amazingly forthright comments. Some said "I don't understand why people don't take out our books. We've got seven copies of Don Quixote." Others wrote that we don't do anything and I wish we did. A few said we have a whole separate Spanish language collection. One most enterprising public librarian in, I think, Sunnyvale, California had made a bilingual pamphlet file by getting pamphlets in English and Spanish from American companies and organizations and packaging them together. This is a great idea.

One library was using something that had come out of the Organization of American States, a list of Spanish language subject headings which the OAS and the Council on Library Resources had put a lot of money into developing. A great many Spanish language librarians, primarily from the countries of Central and South America, spent months arguing over which terms were going to be acceptable to all versions of Spanish and so forth. This was clearly an exciting thing, to know that one library was using this in the United States and that it could be recommended to others.

Then I found that it was out of print. It was unbelievable. It was out of print. I spent a lot of time and some dollars calling up various people I knew at the Organization of American States. They weren't interested. I asked if I could get somebody else willing to publish it, did they have it on negatives or on tape or something so that it could be published fairly easily and would they be willing? They told me they did and they might be willing.

I spoke with various publishers. I called everyone I could think of. I didn't have enough clout. I didn't get anything to happen. I wrote a two page column for the *Wilson Library Bulletin*, describing the survey and deploring the lack of availability of the Spanish language list of subject headings. About a year later there was a letter to the editor of the *Wilson Library Bulletin* from a librarian saying that she had just been able to get from the Organization of American States a Spanish language subject heading list and that they had said it was largely in response to all the noise that Betty Eddison had created. That is change, even if it was totally by accident.

The concept in that project concerning the importance of providing access to information is one that has gone with me wherever I have been. The concept is hardly observed in so much of what we do, because our actions say that unless you read English you don't have access to information in our system, even though we have millions of people who read, but in languages other than English.

I think we're getting a lot better about that. Partly the attitude is improving, even if we don't have subject headings in other languages. At least we are increasingly able to believe that people are not illiterate just because they can't read English. That's something that we have to keep in mind as we are dealing more and more with people who really can't read.

Making Things Happen

The title that was given to this particular segment of today, "The Entrepreneur as Change Agent: Innovation through Product and Service Genesis" is a fine title. I have a slightly shorter one: "Making It Happen." I think that is a very important thing for all of us in the library profession to hang on to.

Certainly as an entrepreneur it is crucial because you realize as you start a company that raising enough money to pay the rent and so forth is pretty important. Raising enough money to pay someone else so that they can pay their rent is even more important — and scary. When you start having a staff of eighteen and twenty and you have to meet that payroll, you definitely have to make a few things happen in order to make sure that life keeps going.

There are all sorts of ways of making things happen. In a public library it can be making sure that enough funding comes in the town or city budget. As an entrepreneur, it can be making sure that you're designing a service or a product that meets a need that the market place is prepared to buy. John Berry, after all, is editor-in-chief of *Library Journal*, a magazine that's highly successful. They're obviously doing something right. There are other magazines that have closed this year. They obviously didn't do something right, or they were too late on the scene and people's loyalties and dollars had gone into other places.

Warner-Eddison Associates, Inc.

When Alice Warner and I were getting ready to graduate from

Simmons, we both were absolutely convinced that we were going to work in community colleges. We were tremendously excited by the initial idea of a community college being a central information referral for an entire community as well as for students, and so forth and so on. Here's where accident comes in again. President Nixon decided to stop federal funding at that point for college libraries. Alice and I were too old and too experienced to start as Librarian I someplace. We were not experienced enough to go in as senior librarians and there were no middle slots around. We looked at each other and we decided we'd better create our own jobs.

That's how we started Warner-Eddison Associates, Inc., the service referred to in the title of this talk.

We learned over time that we were an information management consulting company. We spent most of the next ten years working with American corporations and government agencies, helping them to figure out their information needs and then helping them to meet those needs.

Somebody once asked me if I thought I had made any contribution to the profession and I had to reply that I thought that creating something like eighty jobs that had never existed before for members of my profession was a contribution.

One of the many things that we found as we were consultants to business and industry in the field of information management is that most American leaders in business, industry and government don't have a clue what information tools are available. A few stories will illustrate what I mean.

I was asked by a major architectural firm in Boston to act as consultant. They were building a corporate headquarters for a major corporation and they had been asked to include a corporate library. The architectural firm felt confident when dealing with academic libraries, but they had never built a special library before. That is why they came to me. I said that I would be happy to help if I could meet their clients, find out what their information needs are and talk to them about their information aspirations. This company was sort of camping in a lot of inappropriate buildings while waiting for their fancy new space to be built for them. I looked around, interviewed about ten or twelve people, found out how they used information, what they wanted it for, and so forth and so on. They showed me where they kept their archives. This room had four open doors and they had corporate documents, things that they are required to be able to produce to the SEC at any time, available for the taking. Clearly they needed a different way of keeping track of their archives.

I sat with the architect in a meeting with a number of senior corporate people plus the executive vice president of this corporation. I told him what I thought they needed and in what form. After hearing me through, he looked at me and asked "Is there some way I can get hold of an annual report without having to write to the secretary of the corporation?" I felt like saying, come with me to the Casbah and I will tell you my secrets. But instead I told him about the Disclosure microfiche collection of company reports (this was before the database had been made available). I suggested that they could buy the entire microfiche collection, give it to the business school at the nearby college and make a deal that the business school would send over any microfiche the company wanted to see. Wow, he said, or words to that effect. (We do deal in magic in this profession.)

The change in that organization is going to be absolutely incredible. Their library is going to be three stories high. The downstairs is archives, accessible only through the main floor. The main floor has database searching and periodicals and all the good, normal daily stuff. Everything is accessible internally with stairs, as well as out into the corridors leading to the rest of the corporation. The top floor is for the legal department, where they have study rooms where they can leave all the materials on which they've been working locked in and so on. The new corporate headquarters is getting security for working papers in the law and for the archives, and they are getting access to information that they didn't even know existed. That was being a change agent for them.

Another time I went into the corporate headquarters of a very big corporation. They had asked me to help them put together an internal proposal so that they could have a business information center at corporate headquarters. They had very fancy research centers all over the country at different parts of the company, but this was new corporate headquarters and they had no organized information presence. I told them that I couldn't help them produce their proposal until I went around to see what's what. (I don't know if any of you have ever done this, but if you haven't and you have a chance, try it. When you walk through an organization that doesn't have an organized information presence, i.e., a librarian, you find homemade libraries all over the place. Everyone has what they think they're going to use for their own personal reference needs.)

Squirrel Theory

I went through that process so often that I developed a theory. I often told clients about my squirrel theory. I would say that some day I'm going to write a scholarly paper, and to write a scholarly paper you have to have a theory. I'm going to write about the squirrel theory. I mean this absolutely, desperately, seriously: my squirrel theory is that in any organization people squirrel away the information that they consider vital to their organizational survival.

I have known customers who squirrel away the information they need in the trunks of their cars because that's the place to which only they have access — they are the only people who have the key. I know people who hardly had room to sit in their offices because they had so much information piled up around the walls to the ceiling.

It was a person of that kind who basically provided all of the raw material for a marketing information center that his company asked me to build for them. After I had done that, they called me up one day and asked if I would come down the next week for a meeting. I said, "Surely, but why?" They said, "We want you to present the squirrel of the year award to _____."

I think there was a little malice in their intent. But I decided I was not going to support malice. I presented him with the squirrel of the year award (which their artist had drawn up) and said that if he had not squirreled away all of that information that his company wouldn't have a clue about their corporate competitors. It was his information which provided the raw material for that information center.

It happened over and over again. People who had self-perceived needs for information came to us and said can you help us get a handle on this?

The first library we built was entirely manufacturers' catalogs. It was a design engineering firm and all they needed was access to companies who made the things they needed to put into the machines and buildings they were designing. The reason they came to us was that they had just specified in a proposal (which had been accepted) a piece of machinery that hadn't been made for five years.

We set them up with a catalog library, a vendor catalog library, with a full card catalog including detailed subject access. We didn't try to apply a classification system. We didn't use Library of Congress subject headings. Rather, we used mostly subject headings from Engineering Society. This was organizing information that was valuable for those people to meet their needs.

That is what we did for years and years and years: provide people and organizations with information which was important to them.

Public Libraries

That's one of the things I think that is becoming increasingly important for public libraries. I have recently joined the Board of Library Commissioners in Massachusetts. It was one of Governor Dukakis' last good deeds. Talk about pro bono work! I told them the other day I didn't know I was supposed to take a physical exam before accepting this appointment. The documents we get before every meeting are unbelievable. One of the things in these perilous times that we're going to try to help public libraries to do is to become the special library to the town government of their community, to interview the town management, the environment people, the finance people, the purchasing people, the public works people. In effect, many of our communities have not built a bridge between the public library and the town government. If we're going to make sure that the town government funds the public library, we've got to make sure that the public library is indispensable to the good functioning of the town government. I pass that thought to you. Please do something thereon.

Computers and All That

In terms of the product mentioned in the title, this is a roundabout way to say that all of this experience in dealing with a great many people, analyzing their information needs and producing information tools for them often required production of special catalog cards. If you build a vendor catalog library, you really can't get cards from the Library of Congress. We started out having somebody type every single card. We didn't do the Spencerian handwriting, but we did have all the cards typed. Then we got a little savvier and we typed the first card and had it reproduced. But then you still had to sort them (I need three of these and five of those and four of these and so forth), then the cards had to come back and they all had to go into the typewriter one by one so that the headings could be typed on them. I was getting absolutely frantic because of the inefficiency involved in this approach.

Automatic typewriters were just beginning to come out at that point so I went to a colleague with whom I had worked when we were indexing a lot of manuals for Digital Equipment Corporation. (I knew about indexing and she knew about operating systems on computers.) This time I asked her which automatic typewriter we should get. She looked at me and she said, "Betty, I have watched you now for several years and you guys are changing so fast and doing so many things, why don't you just skip the automatic typewriter stage?" "Skip it," I said. "How?" "Buy a computer." "Buy a computer!" I had visions of white coats and clean rooms and huge machines and large expenses. She said, "No, no. DEC has something they call a micro. It's a PDP 11/03. It's the smallest they make and it's got eight inch floppy disks and 64K memory."

Well, we bought that machine and we had a grown-up operating system called RT-11. We thought it was the cat's meow; clearly we had gotten the best thing in the world. Of course, what I soon found was that I was getting bills for writing different versions of the software so that some people could have their cards with the headings in upper case and other people in lower and upper mixed and other people wanted to do it in yet a different way.

Finally I said, "Let's generalize this thing, okay? So we don't have to keep having all these bills coming in for changes all the time."

Developing a Product

We generalized and we generalized and before long the software was working pretty well. Then our clients heard about the fact that we had this software and a couple of them called up and asked if they couldn't have it to put on their computers. We thought for quite some time about developing a product, which is what we would have to do if we were to provide it to our clients.

We thought and we thought and we decided, yes, we would offer this software as a product. Therefore we did all the things that you need to do to take something that's for the family, so to speak, and turn it into something for the public, and we started selling it. But we were still running an information management consulting company and we had never had any outside funding. (We still have never had any outside funding, so it's been sweat equity galore.) But it got to be a little tricky. We couldn't do enough consulting to finance the ongoing development and support of the software product. At this point the software was working on DEC PDP-11 computers under a variety of operating systems and on DEC VAXs.

In 1983 when the PC and MS-DOS came along in a big way, we had to decide where we were. We decided we would have a product for the PC. At the same time we decided we would stop consulting and would assign all the value of the software and so forth to a new company. We decided we would give the new company the name of our product.

Inmagic, Inc

Since December 1983 the company has been Inmagic, Inc. Our flagship product runs under MS-DOS, and on DEC VAX's. We have customers in some fifty-seven countries. Ours is the most widely used software in special libraries in Canada. (We know that because the *Canadian Library Journal* does a survey every year.) We think we have the most used software in the United States as well, based on a variety of measures, but we don't have hard numbers on that.

Use of our products in public and academic libraries is for the third stage of automation. It's for when people want the flexibility to be able to do whatever they want to do without having to learn a programming language and all kinds of things. The public library in Los Angeles has decided on our product as their software of choice. They have multiple copies in different departments all over the LA Public Library for a variety of their special needs (a thirty thousand record database about their photograph collection, etc.). Yale University has multiple copies of our product, not for their housekeeping stuff, but in the Divinity School, in the Beinecke Rare Book library, and so forth. The Yale Forestry School uses it and has taken one copy to their forestry project in Nepal.

In special libraries our products have made it possible for librarians and others to be change agents in their organizations, to provide access to information for the organization, information which makes the organization able to function more strongly. Some of our customers have been such effective change agents that they have earned new titles and new salaries.

Being a Change Agent

Perhaps being a change agent is part of being a continuum of change. As you can see, it all happened by accident. I am a change agent. I know I am. But it wasn't because I sat down and said, I will be a change agent. It's because opportunities keep sliding under the door, or in the window, or over the transom, and if you recognize them and they fit where you are that day, you can march forward. That does make for change. We have a marvelous profession. It's one of the most creative groups of people I have ever seen. The only limits that we have are because we haven't looked far enough around the next corner. We really can do anything we want.

The Administrator as Change Agent: Reshaping Organizations, Questioning Old Verities and Sharing the Blame

Charles W. Robinson

I'm not sure at all that I'm the person to talk about "The Administrator as Change Agent." I'm not really very accustomed to change, and I'm not even sure I like it very much: I've had the same wife for thirty-five years, I've lived in the same house for twenty-five years (yes, the mortgage, for $134.00 a month, is paid off), I've worked in the same public library for thirty-two years, and I've been director for twenty-eight years, not because I haven't applied for other jobs, but because I have been turned down for every job I've applied for since 1959. There are not many people who have had that practically unblemished record of mud-sticking in this profession or any other profession.

On the other hand, just being unqualified to speak on a subject has never seemed to deter me. I have talked at a number of places around the country, and written some articles, on the subject of collection development, or book selection. It has occurred to me recently, however, that in forty years since I graduated from library school, I have *never* selected a book. I once did order some books from a Baker and Taylor exhibit at an ALA conference, but after I got back to the library, the coordinator of materials selection told me that she had canceled the order and I was not to do that again.

From what I read, and from the various professional institutes and seminars I have been to in recent years, the whole subject of organizational change has become about as fashionable in academia and in management self-help books as designer water in a fern bar. There must be scores of academics—probably some right here at Rutgers (maybe even in the library school?)—who have made intensive studies of the subject, conducted research, written lengthy articles, perhaps even some with equations, little Greek letters, pie charts, and circles with arrows pointing up, down and sideways. From that point of view, we administrators, or practitioners, don't know a hell of a lot about change, innovation, reshaping organizations. Academics will be able to talk and write rings around us—especially us public librarians, who, you may have observed, do very little writing.

Public library directors are little potentates in many cases: they run their own organizations and are responsible, unlike directors of most academic libraries, for almost every facet of administration, from technical services (a subject which, with their brand of collection development, seems to take up about 90 percent of the time of an academic library director) to personnel, the tax rate, local politics, plumbing, the homeless, personnel problems, buildings, parking,and if there's time, some of the subjects learned in library school, such as information services and "age-level specialists," whatever they are, or pretend to be.

In other words, we don't think anywhere nearly as much about organizational change as we do about changes in the budget, and, more seriously, we don't think hardly at all about public library philosophy. It's really difficult to run a public library *effectively* if you, your staff, and your board don't know what a public library is supposed to do. In other words, if you don't decide on a clear mission.

It's very easy to run a public library *ineffectively* if you don't know your mission, or if the mission tries to do everything, or if the mission is so fuzzy it's really unclear. And this is the way that most public libraries are managed—ineffectively. Often very comfortably, I admit, but ineffectively. We are very, very lucky public administrators in that public libraries are about as important to the general public as the local car wash emporium (the industry of public libraries is just about the same size as the car wash industry in this country). We can be just as fuzzy about our mission and just as comfortable in our offices as we want to—nobody really notices. And that, currently and over the past forty years, has been our salvation.

I'm constantly involved in organizational change. You are too, or you soon will be. But, I seldom think about ORGANIZATIONAL CHANGE as an entity in itself, the way that academics can and do. And, thanks to these same academics, who appear at seminars and workshops, I can gain some insights, some knowledge, and some realization of how my staff and I can avoid some really stupid mistakes. One good thing about the approach of geezerhood is the recognition that, as Drucker says, if you want people to perform in an organization, you have to use their strengths (including your own, I assume), not emphasize their weaknesses. I have plenty of weaknesses, but I'm a pretty good administrator in some areas. The academics have helped me strengthen these areas, but nothing they can do will eliminate some of my weaknesses. Acceptance comes with geezerhood, you'll be glad to learn.

Let's pay some attention to these academics: the other day, I heard a very, very good talk from Mark Roberts, the director, or dean, or whatever, of the Kennedy School of Political Science at Harvard. Dr. Roberts gave a couple of good anecdotal examples (we practitioners give a lot more credence to anecdotal evidence than we do to statistical evidence) of how hard it is to change organizational behavior.

1. One of the most effective new high-tech weapons used in the Gulf War was the new breed of artillery—the multiple launch rocket-propelled projectiles, designed to cover a broad area with a lot of explosive power. Artillerymen were loath to adopt this technology, for some very good reasons of organizational culture. The artillery is, as we all know, a very traditional part of the Army ("Hi, Hi, Hee, for the Field Artillery"): each unit has a boss (the highest ranking officer), uniforms, isolation from the infantry and the armor, self-containment, prizes, stories, training, songs, flags, etc. All the stories, all the successes, revolve around putting shells in exactly the right spot: accuracy.

Multiple launch missiles are very, very effective, but pinpoint accuracy is not a strength, not a necessity. Let's not adopt them!

2. Another story: the top men in utilities are almost always engineers or lawyers. When an engineer was the boss, the utility company was almost always less successful in meeting environmental concerns than companies where a lawyer was the boss. Why? Engineers are trained that there is a right answer and a wrong answer to every problem. They spend years checking all the mathematical formulas for this and that, and they serve as consultants to each other on various projects, just as we librarians do, by the way. If an environmental group wants to talk about problems, engineers are not prone to discuss them—after all, what's wrong about what's presently being done? We've figured it all out!

Lawyers, now, are really negotiators by trade. They all hate to go to trial—they might lose! Lawyers argue—that argument often leads to negotiation, and lawyers are quite ready to meet with the environmental groups and very often arrive at some mutual accommodation. So they are more successful in running these utilities than the engineers.

Some librarians tend toward the culture of engineers: they love order, tend to abhor ambiguity, and are often detailists who see things in terms of black and white, right or wrong. Those of you who are familiar with the Meyers-Briggs personality indicator must have thought about the fact that these indicators show that while 70 percent of the population as a whole tend to be extroverts, 70 percent of librarians tend to be introverts. That obviously has some effect on organizational culture in libraries.

Ron Dubberly, the director of the Atlanta-Fulton Public Library, and one of the few public library directors who thinks a lot about public librarianship and public library philosophy, called me the other day and reported that he had given a talk at FSU about "paradigm shifters." "What the hell is *that*?" I asked, remembering that at one time I knew what a paradigm was, but that I had forgotten. Ron explained that a paradigm was a set of rules, and that paradigm shifters were described by one Joel Barker, in a book titled *Discovering the Future—The Business of Paradigms* (St. Paul, MN: ILI Press, 1985).

Barker explains that a paradigm shifter is, simply, an outsider. In science, the person who is most likely to begin to create new rules, rather than just apply the old rules is from one of two backgrounds—

1. A young graduate, newly out of school, who has been trained in the field but has not practiced in it.

2. An older scientist who is shifting fields—say from chemistry to biology.

The quality that both share is *operational naivete* about the field, and they lack investment in the old paradigm, or set of rules about the field. There's a third kind of paradigm shifter, and that's a *tinkerer*, who just works on problems which have become important to him or her, ignoring the paradigms of the field, like the computer programmer who invented Visicalc, knowing little about accounting.

All of these types are, of course, change agents, and we have people like them—not very many it is true—in the field of library administration; or collection development, or cataloging, or what have you. And they all, to one extent or another, challenge, or more realistically, ignore the conventional wisdom. Conventional wisdom should not, of course, be ignored by everyone (if so, it wouldn't be conventional, of course), because, after all, it's wisdom. And it's a good thing that not everyone is a paradigm shifter, or we wouldn't have any paradigm, or wisdom, at all.

I'm really suspicious of paradigm shifters, or rather, the attempts at shifting paradigms, by people in any field, but especially in the field of librarianship, where I feel secure. But I'm mostly suspicious of myself and frankly, my staff, who, for good or ill, have garnered for the Baltimore County Public Library a reputation for craziness, questioning old verities, and — if you will — shifting paradigms. That's a reputation that's not always easy to live with, especially under the attack of the personification of the conventional wisdom of the sixties, John Berry. Luckily for us, however, he has let the camel's nose into the tent, so to speak, in the person of Nora Rawlinson, former paradigm shifter at BCPL. Luckily for the profession, Nora, while also a child of the sixties, has grown up. I think. Maybe.

Now that I've proved the incredible value of the master's degree I earned in 1951 by quoting the academics, what do I really think about change, since I've apparently been invited here under the guise of a change agent? Well, I've already said I'm not fond of it, which is not quite true — I'm really fond of change I create myself, or that I approve of beforehand. I just don't like change that's imposed on me by others — and believe me, that happens a lot. But I haven't always been a great change causer, either. We administrators are almost always ridden by insecurities and are terrified of making moves which cause us to be criticized, especially by the library press. This attitude, of course, only encourages the inaccurate and scurrilous attacks of the press. I really believe in the freedom of the press, except in the case of attacks on me or my library. But, that's the penalty of having the reputation of a change agent, however undeserved.

My staff, however, or at least some of them, really deserve the reputation — and let me tell you why.

Lowell Martin, whom we honor here today, and who did a lot to put the Baltimore County Public Library on its present road of public service, did a survey for BCPL in 1957, titled *Library Service for Baltimore County*. This survey was my bible when I joined BCPL as assistant director in 1959. Lowell, along with his co-consultants, Mary Gaver and James Bryan, also luminaries in the field at that time, gave detailed recommendations for the library's growth in both collections and facilities. For the first five years, working under the highly professional and personally competent guidance of the director, Richard D. Minnich, we labored to fulfill the plan in every detail — a labor which met with a high degree of success, and which forms the foundation, at least in some important ways, of the present library service. I don't think we could have done it without Lowell Martin's help and his clear long-range plan. Of course, he was the expert from across the state line with a briefcase, but he provided the vision – sometimes a rare thing when one is fully occupied with the exigencies of a growing demand and inadequate support of dollars.

In 1963, the director died and I was appointed director, yes, as simple as that: no search committees, long interregnum or anything like what is customary today. Realizing some of my inadequacies, which wasn't difficult, the board and I went out and dragooned Jean-Barry Molz, who had experience both in administration and in branch management at the Pratt Library in Baltimore, to be deputy director.

You couldn't find two more traditionally-minded librarians at that time – we had both had our first work experience in large metropolitan libraries, I in Philadelphia and she in Baltimore, and worked under respected directors, people like Emerson Greenaway, Ed Castagna, and Joe Wheeler, all ALA bigwigs. We worshipped Lowell Martin, who had also done an important series of studies for the Pratt, the Deiches Studies, and we tried, really tried, not only to run a good, growing library system for the people of Baltimore County, but to run a library which would have the respect of the profession.

Then something happened. Slowly, at first, and then for a number of reasons, with a rush – a rush which hasn't yet seemed to properly die down and run its course, so to speak.

The collection development paradigms which we had learned at the feet of our mentors in Philadelphia and Baltimore, and reinforced by Lowell Martin, didn't work. We couldn't hire enough librarians with the MLS degree to meet the requirements of new buildings. The staff we hired were almost all young, new to the profession, and asked questions of us for which we were unprepared by the conventional wisdom. The conventional organization of staff didn't work under the impact of explosive growth of circulation, again with insufficient dollars to hire enough staff to meet conventional standards. Traditional methods of materials selection and the leisurely approach to book processing kept books from reaching the public – a public, which you will remember, to whom we had promised good service.

We were desperate. We took stomach pills until we discovered that no one knew how desperate we were. But being desperate didn't make the problems go away, or the staff from looking to us for answers, answers which they were perfectly willing to supply when we couldn't.

Jean-Barry and I aren't really the best in the world at any one thing we do, except one, and at that we are magnificient, by which I mean we're absolutely right 60 percent of the time: hiring good staff. Of course, our technique gets us into trouble, too. We like people who think for themselves and who don't really buy *all* the paradigms of the profession, and when hiring a new professional, one of our standard questions was "What would you do with a copy of the *Odyssey* in your branch if you found it hadn't circulated in three years?" What we wanted for an answer, of course, was something like a semi-agonized "I'd discard it," showing that this candidate was more interested in books for people to read than in the custodial concept of a keeper of the Western literary tradition. But in a sense, it's a trick question: the *Odyssey does* circulate, if only because it's often assigned to students by keepers of the Western literary tradition, professors and teachers. When this question was quoted in an article in 1978 in *Publishers Weekly*, however, an uproar was created in the library community: "Baltimore County doesn't have the *Odyssey* in its libraries! Horrors!," or, a description of BCPL as the "bookstore library," an inaccurate depiction still widely held in the profession.

We had stepped on a paradigm. We had before, when we had, in self-defense, sort of invented the short-entry catalog, in order to save money on paper for our computer-prepared book catalog in 1964 (four years before MARC). That little exercise earned me the angry comment by a professor of cataloging from Rutgers in a Palmer House bar: "You have set cataloging back fifty years!" He vanished before I could defend myself, which was probably impossible given his paradigms, but I felt really guilty. For a while. Incidentally, we *still* have a short-entry catalog, but it's on CD. My daughter, a sales representative for CLSI, says we're out of step with the profession because we don't have an online catalog. I knew I should have discouraged her from going to library school!

Probably the most serious rule we broke, for which we have hardly been criticized at all, was the creation of a class of paraprofessionals we call "library associates." We created the class of 1963, first taught by another subversive rule-breaker, Thomas Walker, then of our state library agency, who also participated in the inspiration of our notorious centralized materials selection scheme. In any event, these library associates now comprise about 60 percent of our information desk staff, and they don't have the MLS! We also have no trouble hiring MLS's should we need them (we very seldom do), because these paraprofessionals are always sneaking off and getting their library degrees on a part-time basis. We have a built-in supply.

That's not the heresy, though. The heresy is that we have now found out that you don't need a library degree to work effectively and efficiently in a public library. There are thousands of people all across the country behind information desks that prove it. Yes, there are some that are awful, but some of these have the MLS.

I wondered about this until I determined through a fifteen-second research project, that the need to have an MLS to work effectively in a library is a creation of academic politics. In order to have the grudging respect of your colleagues in academia, you've got to have an advanced degree. In the thirties, a master's was relatively advanced and that's when the American Library Association, in league with academic libraries, decreed the necessity for an MLS. Pretty soon now, it looks as if the minimum will be a doctorate. It's certainly now required for any kind of respect, for an academic library directorship, and probably soon for admission to the faculty club.

But public libraries aren't academia, and we don't need the academic trappings. I'll buy the bachelor's degree because that generally is in the liberal arts and doesn't involve the sin of specialization, the hallmark of the doctorate — and sometimes of the master's.

You'll hear a lot of stuff in this profession of how sacred the librarian is, and how important. The American Library Association recently, under the well-intentioned push of the president, Richard Dougherty, an academic librarian, and the president-elect, Pat Schuman, an academic publisher, recently inaugurated the "Decade of the Librarian." This program will elevate the status of librarians, gain them much-needed respect, recognize that libraries are "crucial" to progress and, not the least, raise their salaries. Let me tell you a secret: ALA has been trying to do this for at least fifty years. I looked at the salary reports of libraries published in the *ALA Bulletin* (now *American Libraries*) for 1940, applied the CPI since then, and came out with what librarians are getting paid today. I started in 1953 in Philadelphia for $3,583. Apply the CPI to that figure and you'll get about $26,000, just about the starting salary for a librarian today. I took the salary of the executive director of ALA in 1940, and now, and it's almost exactly the same. And also for what then was the director of PLA. And I also took the charts done by Amy Winslow, who was the head of the salary committee of ALA at at that time — same as now. No progress in fifty years. Bad news. If you think the "Decade of the Librarian" is going to change it, think again. Also, if you're in the business for current money, think again. Of course, if you're in it for the pension forty years from now, I'll tell you another secret: you'll be rich.

Along with the heresy that not all people manning information desks must possess the MLS—possibly just the administrators, the trainers, and some specialists—we adopted another heresy, that all public service librarians and paraprofessionals should be generalists. That is, that they should be trained to serve, at least adequately, all age levels. With this action, of course, we eliminated all age-level specialists, and even the support of the administrative staff was divided among collection development people and information people, rather than the traditional adult, young adult and children's coordinators.

In truth, this was merely a recognition of how most public libraries operate, rather than how they are organized. In most small and medium-sized libraries, and certainly in the community branches of the new poor, the large city libraries, there are not enough staff members to take assignments at the separate adult and children's desks at some times, and the service demands vary considerably at each desk depending upon the time of day. Better service overall is a direct result of having staff who are trained to serve at either desk as the situation demands. In addition, the utilization of staff among agencies, on staff committees and for other assignments is greatly simplified when specialized titles and job descriptions are eliminated.

Unlike the much more serious step of reducing the need for MLS-degree librarians, which has created no more than a ripple in the profession, BCPL's adoption of the generalist plan has created howls from children's librarians, who apparently have a very serious problem with recognition, or self-esteem, or something.

Anyway, generalism works, and works very well, because it serves the public use of libraries more efficiently than specialization. Interestingly, you don't have to encourage librarians to specialize—they always will. You *do* have to encourage them to be generalists.

All of this, of course, has to do with reshaping organizations, but that's not the point: organizations have to be shaped, first, to carry out your mission, and second, to fit the strengths of the staff you have. One of the most frustrating things I see often in libraries is the tendency to draw up organization plans without considering the abilities of the staff you have.

But, of course, the most basic issue is identification of mission, and that's where the Baltimore County Public Library has, in my personal opinion, contributed most to helping us all to a more thorough understanding of the place public libraries have in our society.

Let's consider that the philosophy of library service runs on a continuum, from the preservation and custodial instincts of the research or academic library at one end of the scale, to pure service to the public at the other end of the scale, without consideration of materials as artifacts, but rather as commodities which are necessary for information transfer or recreational reading. The problem with public library philosophy at the present time is that we are confused as to where on this continuum we belong. It's a problem because we cannot afford to do it all, and when we try, as we almost always do, we fail along the whole continuum.

In addition, we are confused and our service is hobbled by sentimental or moralistic views of library service. Probably the best example of this is in our professional association, where endless resolutions are passed about the image of librarians, the sanctity of access for all, gulf wars, the homeless, preservation, acid-free paper, government information, and what not, all of which tends to confuse the people trying to give people books they want when they want them at a cost, whether in taxes or fees, which they are willing to pay. Public libraries should be concerned with service, not collection-building, and service to the people who exist *now*, not those who might exist in the future, or, more likely in our present thinking, those who we wish *did* exist, at least in numbers it would be economical to serve.

Unfortunately, those of us who administer public libraries must deal with the paradigms of the profession—a profession which is controlled in our professional association, and in the minds of many of our trustees, and in our professional literature, by the academic mystique, overlaid by moralistic pronouncements of the importance of libraries to democracy, the economy, the environment, the social fabric, mental health, the status of women, safe sex, the importance of oat bran, and any other cause in which any member of the profession is currently interested.

I would hope that change in public libraries is tending toward a recognition of serving the people, instead of serving a profession whose responsibilities and interests are much broader than ours need to be or should be. If recognition of our mission and implementation of policies and practices to fulfill that mission in a practical and cost-efficient manner bring big changes to public libraries, then we will really serve as the public's library.

At the Baltimore County Public Library, we have gone from being a traditional, collection-centered institution to that of a more service-oriented institution, although there are still, at least from the point of view of most of our staff, areas where improvements can be made, dozens of them.

We are starting with what works, and building our policies from that. We are letting the public we serve design the shoes for us to walk in, not the profession, not the library press, and most of all, not we ourselves.

Who's *we*? Not me, not our trustees, not Jean-Barry Molz, not our administrative council. All of us, together and separately, and we all share the blame. There are those who see BCPL as a change agent. We are not. But we have found that Tom Peters is right in some of his maxims of pop management — a form of management information which is probably twice as effective as speeches like this or papers from schools of business management:

- Anything worth doing is worth doing poorly (remember the first phone and airplane);
- Ask dumb questions;
- Pursue failure — failure is success's only launching pad;
- Root out "not invented here." Swipe from the best;
- Constantly reorganize;
- Listen to everyone;
- Share all information in-house. No secrets.

The whole staff is responsible for change. So, of course, are plenty of people from outside our library. Even John Berry, who keeps us honest, keeps us thinking.

I would hope that the students here are troublemakers in their institution too — realistically, I know that only some of you will be. Not everyone can or should shift paradigms — and not all paradigms should be shifted. But public libraries, more than any other kind of libraries today, have the largest collection of paradigms which need changing — and no one is going to do it except you.

The Profession as Change Agent: The Bandwagon Effect*

John N. Berry III

Librarians have been subjected to a host of causes. We are an over-organized and relatively militant profession. Our organizational reality, as Charlie pointed out, is almost the opposite of our public image. As you have heard today, we have a variety of leaders and styles of leadership. We can be enlisted in causes, and when the marching orders are given, we line up and step out, and often we do accomplish change. Jana Varlejs put the phrase, "the bandwagon effect," at the end of a longer title when she gave me this assignment. I was troubled at first, but upon reflection I believe this bandwagon effect is a major way that the organized library profession serves as its own change agent. I have used "bandwagon effect" to describe the phenomenon, because whether or not that description is accurate, it gives me a wonderful new metaphor to extend and mix with the other metaphors like parades and music and destinations and the like — all of it in the big top of our professional circus.

Whether we are led by bandwagons or not, there is clear evidence of our enlistment in a host of causes, many of them highly abstract to say the least. There are bandwagons and circus parades in every field. The big parades often lead to change. You heard earlier about the bandwagons of business management. You know many of them, as I do — quality circles, zero-based budgeting, empowerment, deregulation, decentralization, a variety of those Japanese management models, and I think that Peter Drucker himself is a management bandwagon. So are Lee Iacocca, Tom Peters, Blanchard, and Rosabeth Kanter.

I am very fearful of Kanter as editor of the *Harvard Business Review*, which has generated more management bandwagons probably than any publication in history. Kanter, as you know, was an economic adviser to Michael Dukakis, a bandwagon that did not get as far as some of the others that she had been related to.

I remember the rental car gurus, although I have forgotten their names; there were the bandwagons of leveraged buyouts and junk bonds and free trade. I even remember one I was subjected to called the Hay Plan, where they put you on grids and measured your performance.

But this is not my turf. Even though I can name that number of bandwagons, I don't know the business best sellers this season, each of which harbors bandwagon potential, I am sure.

Still, consider not only the impact on our society, but the damage that some of these business bandwagons have done as they have careened across America. There is the junk-bond-caused savings and loan crisis, there is the good old Lockheed bailout, the Chrysler bailout, the Japanese share of market problem, the recession, the airline industry, and the phone company. Look at health and medicine—the number of bandwagons that are in collision with each other, like the cholesterol-vitamin-protein wars, or the case of ibuprofen, which is good for arthritis, but will give you ulcers. Or that new anti-cholesterol drug that gives you cataracts and liver problems and other more original side effects. Or the antibiotic craze and the overuse of them that created wonderful new immune bacteria to plague us all. The doctors now say no meat of any kind at all if you can avoid it—no chicken, no fish, no veal, no beef—nada, except as rarest treats in your steady diet of a few beans, some grains and other uncooked vegetables and a little fruit. Or look at child rearing—the bandwagons in parenting—those Spock-marked kids, as *Time* once called them.

What are the characteristics of a bandwagon? Those who disagree with the directions taken by movements or the zeal with which they are pursued, are likely to label new crusades and efforts to be the results of a bandwagon effect. For the converted, however, to be accused of following a bandwagon is a pejorative attack designed to trivialize the cause and suggest that its adherents are too shallow and too stupid to figure out that it is only a pretty bandwagon at the head of a parade, noisy and colorful but probably unknowingly headed for only obsolescence, irrelevance or oblivion.

Those involved and converted to the cause see their actions differently, as crusades for change—courageous efforts by a small minority who by capturing the imagination of the main stream start a professional movement in our field. Those ideas sometimes harden into the credo of a professional ideology or religion. You know many of the elements of the religion of librarians — what Robert Leigh and the people who did The Public Library Inquiry in the fifties called "The Library Faith." You probably agree with many of its tenets, as I do. They center on the book: we are the people of the book, the people of learning, and archives. We have been celebrated by Ray Bradbury and Asimov, most college presidents, immigrants, and of course ourselves.

We are the unrecognized saviors of civilization and humanity, ever vigilant to fight off the barbarian hordes, who will deaden our brains with television, kill our institutions by refusing to pay taxes, and in general ruin our society by not paying sufficient tribute to the book, booklearning, reading — the things we hold most dear. So when that cause or idea, that great administrative, entrepreneurial, or organizational inspiration matures and gains followers, it is often transformed from an innovation into an ornate bandwagon sounding off at full volume. That bandwagon starts to lead one of our professional parades. As it moves, it changes. The nature and ownership of the cause changes, it becomes everybody's. Then the committees and the task forces and the volunteer busybodies begin to reshape it. At best, as in the case of our position on censorship, that bandwagon becomes a part of our faith, our ideology, and our religion. When that happens, it then transcends any lesser cause and all causes forever after are measured against that sacred one.

We ask now of every innovation in the library field, does it conform to our scripture, our Library Bill of Rights?

In a wonderfully insightful dissertation for her Columbia Ph.D. (*Forbidden Books in American Public Libraries, 1876-1939*, Greenwood Press, 1984), Evelyn Geller studied how we became so absolutely opposed to censorship. It's a wonderful lesson in bandwagons and change. She found that the idea actually developed as an unanticipated consequence of debates in early library history about whether or not libraries should collect fiction at all. One side said fiction was trash, an abject appeal to the popular taste (sounds familiar, doesn't it?). The other side said some fiction was legitimate literature. Ultimately, both wisely decided it was appropriate to have some fiction in libraries. Then began an endless series of arguments about which fiction was appropriate. This led them into a corner: no one could agree and those who came on too strongly really did sound like a lot of censors. The ultimate result was unanticipated but predictable. They decided that no one was qualified to decide which books were appropriate, and this hardened into a very strong position for intellectual freedom and against censorship. The bandwagon had begun.

When that bandwagon is invoked now, everybody joins up and marches in that parade — everybody. That position is never, never questioned. It may have been the earliest beginning of that "give-them-what-they-want" theory of collection development that you just heard espoused so passionately.

The most important characteristic of bandwagon leadership however is this: Whoever is driving that bandwagon is usually far more interested in building a following and having a great parade over which to exercise leadership than in arriving at any particular destination. For the bandwagon, after all, it is the quality of the parade and its audience that counts. The bandwagon leader wants to know the number of people in and the variety of the following, the attention the parade can command — not the destination. Another important characteristic of bandwagon leadership is that the program often takes the parade to someplace different from the destination selected by the original leader. The parade frequently takes a different route from the leader, or changes the nature of the leader's mission.

Goal displacement is common and frequent for those parades that follow bandwagons. Today's pitch for management by objectives is tomorrow's output measures. Today's systems concept is tomorrow's multitype library system. Today's resource sharing is tomorrow's RLIN and the next day's National Research and Education Network (NREN). Today's "instruction in library use" is tomorrow's "bibliographic instruction" and the next day's "information literacy." And so it goes, as Kurt Vonnegut so wonderfully describes the process of things.

The third characteristic of bandwagon leadership, related to goal displacement, is that often what leaders actually start in more deliberate processes, turn quickly into bandwagons. Look at the primrose path of strategic management down which Brooke Sheldon took ALA. Or watch Dick Dougherty at the head of that NREN parade! Often the enthusiasm is justified. But sometimes, alas, it is just propaganda, like our frequent defenses of the book. Remember Daniel Boorstin's wonderfully compelling defense of knowledge versus information, defense of the book against other formats. Knowledge has no enemies, books have no enemies — there was no battle to be fought over that.

Bandwagons are often fueled by entrepreneurial genius like the leadership that Betty Eddison was discussing. I'm very proud to sit in the chair occupied once by one such entrepreneur, the famous Melvil

Dewey, who gave us a number of very fine parades, the sum of which are still marching about in our profession. For example, there is the notion that the graduate department of a research university is the true and proper site for the education and training of librarians. We probably should give the leadership wreath for creating that bandwagon to Charles C. Williamson.

Bandwagons often take over organizations, too. Look how bandwagons related to type of library and type of activity have produced militant ALA units and divisions, and how they have changed the face and structure of the American Library Association. ALA is now much more important for the activities of its specialist divisions than as a unified organization itself. As a matter of fact, Marilyn Miller, who is the 1992–93 ALA president, says that there is no ALA any more. To the leaders of an ACRL or an AASL or a PLA, ACRL and AASL and PLA are more important. It's always been that way with the school librarians. We should keep in mind, though, the history of movements like that and remember that it was here in New Jersey that John Cotton Dana invented the Special Libraries Association. Very near his death he said he really regretted it, because in fact it had fragmented librarianship into specialist organizations.

The point I'm making here, however, is that organization leaders in those divisions started a bandwagon for each one and their parade has consistently grown until those divisions really now do everything that ALA ever did and do most of it a little better. The people in that parade will never be as numerous, but their loyalty to ACRL or PLA is unswerving.

The same kind of group dynamics exist in ALA as in any group with ties of similarity of purpose or demographics or interest. When the central body gets too big, too difficult to manipulate, or makes it too difficult for a would-be leader to assume leadership, things begin to come apart, to form into more manageable constituencies or splinters. The frustrated leader can then find a place and a group to lead in one of the splinters. ALA has always had this kind of fragmentation problem so people vote for leaders by block, always have. The blocks could be geography, or sex, or type of library or type of service. They were often simply age and sex.

The growing power of the ALA divisions gave more leaders more opportunity to lead, more bandwagons. The bandwagons multiplied as that change took hold, and now an ALA president, over the whole organization, is very hard pressed to accomplish anything. Dana's nightmare has in fact come true: ALA is a paper tiger.

Charlie Robinson here today is a good example: Charlie's petition campaign to be president of PLA was successful, while his petition campaign to be president of ALA was not. Charlie has devoted a great deal of his creative organizational energies to PLA with tremendous payoff for that organization. No question about it, the recent PLA conference in San Diego was great. ALA could have used Charlie's energies and genius more broadly but his constituency was trapped in public libraries. Bandwagons started by Charlie has given us a large number of very fine parades.

As you can see, my own prejudices allow me to label as bandwagon effects several of the past and present fashions of modern librarianship. Some of you will be able to guess which movements I would so demean, but for those who don't, let me list a few more, and try to discuss and describe them in terms that are useful to our understanding of change and leadership and all those things we are supposed to be discussing.

I have to mention Charlie again. His theory of public library book selection was a fine parade — *is* a fine parade — indeed, now pursued as a crusade by those who are converted to it, not the least of whom is my esteemed colleague at *Library Journal*, Nora Rawlinson, the acquisitions librarian I pirated away from Baltimore County. She and her centralized book selection cadres threw a number of very compelling programs at the PLA conference in San Diego.

There is a whole fleet of bandwagons emerging from the overarching idea that the best models for managing libraries come from the literature of practice and theory of business management. That crowd of MBA-style librarians and vendors, like Bill Sannwald at San Diego Public, Tony Leisner at Quality Books, and even Ann Prentice in the good old days before, alas, she became an academic administrator, and a host of others — they brought you the bandwagon of marketing in libraries. There was the library as free bookstore. There were output measures and a variety of budgeting and participatory management schemes. There was a veritable host of well meaning but misguided attempts to answer that age-old question that always comes out when some self-important business manager looks at libraries for the first time and says, "Why don't they run it like a business?"

They always ask that question. In the last two weeks I have made calls in Toronto; St. Louis; San Diego; Juneau; Cromwell, Connecticut; New Brunswick, New Jersey. I have been repeatedly asked that damnable question. I have begun to fear that there is a whole new queue of "run-it-like-a-business" bandwagons right around the corner, waiting for this spring or the next to start a host of new parades to seduce us all.

One of these business types, for example, has signed up exclusive licenses with a major database vendor group and now will proceed to try to convince libraries that only if they will accept this fee schedule, this little fee for service, for database searches he can provide electronic information through the library to its terminals, or to the homes of library card holders. He will become central then to the new information age, an age in which he sees libraries as marginal. This guy sees a huge potential market, with libraries, of course, as a ready-made distribution channel for the service he wants to sell. This bandwagon will play "join-the-information-age" music when the parade begins, and of course the poor, and the print-oriented library users will as usual be given wonderful seats on the curb when that parade rolls by.

Do people care? Charlie said they didn't. I can only cite that wonderful Lou Harris poll, released at the PLA meeting in San Diego, which replaces the old Gallup one that gave us pretty good numbers. This one says 65 percent of the people use the public library on a frequent and regular basis. I think that's a lot of caring. These were all people, incidentally, over the age of eighteen.

I met a man in Toronto last week who rose to company president from his beginnings as a computer jockey. Of course he complained to me that, "They ought to run the library like a business." "They don't run it like a business because it is not a business," I said as I fired a salvo of hostile questions at him: "Besides, which business shall we take as a model? Banks and savings and loans? Air travel? The wonderfully competitive American automobile industry? Stock brokerages, like Drexel Burnham Lambert? Library automation? Farming? Lumber? How about telephone and telecommunication? Maybe the *Daily News*."

Even some of our most cherished professional beliefs have the look or sound of the bandwagon. Consider Melvil Dewey's idea that all the knowledge of mankind is conveniently and endlessly divisible by ten. There's a crackpot idea, a bandwagon notion that has sent librarianship plummeting down the escarpment of hierarchy and classification for a century or more now. How about that automation bandwagon that passed through the field some time back in the costume of those early turnkey library systems? CLSI was the first, I guess, the one that came closest to becoming a bandwagon at the beginning.

The crashes of that automation bandwagon as it careened through our field are notable. Some librarians — Charlie was not among that crowd — forced CLSI to add functions way beyond what a fairly good circulation system could handle. They are recovering now by adding functions and power to the product. But the product of course now is a whole different product, the online public access catalog. The bandwagon of automated systems included many brand names we remember, like Dataphase, already piled up in that library automation junkyard.

Automation taught us something else about bandwagons. Their advocates and bettors don't always have a clear purpose in mind. Early experiments with libraries and technology were notably diffuse, yet they created the imperative to automate libraries in whatever way they could be automated. This launched a very productive era of at least three or four decades of innovation, experimentation, and real growth. What the library automation movement created was the machinery that solved modern problems of information organization, management, and delivery.

I think that the next bandwagon will have to be the one that insures that all citizens will have full, free access to this magic. That bandwagon, incidentally, is already beginning to lumber up to the starting point of the parade at our professional meetings now. I want to be in that parade and I hope that you will all be in it too. I hope that parade comes very soon.

We are here to honor Lowell Martin, and we have all mentioned him. Let's examine a bandwagon or two that he drove. The most important Martin bandwagon is role setting for public libraries. I think the value of this one is still unproven. In two or three years we really ought to know how it has turned out. I remember Martin's consultant report to the Free Library of Philadelphia. It became the Bowker lecture that was mentioned earlier. The recommendations included Martin's famous exhortation to that library to "concentrate and strengthen." He said that the Philadelphia Free Library could not be everything to everyone and that it should select a few roles that it could play well. Elliot Shelkrot, the current director of the Philadelphia Free Library, a known card-carrying Robinson protégé and mentee, has just issued an annual report that spells out four roles that the Free Library of Philadelphia has selected. The centerpiece of the whole PLA planning process is a reflection of Martin's role setting. That idea has its roots, incidentally, in the marketing literature of business. In business they call it "market segmentation." When they do it, however, they decide *not* to meet certain needs or demands that are out there. It remains to be seen, I think, whether or not public libraries can justify that kind of role setting. If it is true, as Charlie says, that the citizens really are going to decide what the place is for, fine. The old Philadelphia Free Library, however, has not fared well since that Martin report. Its troubles we hope are mostly political and so far unrelated to the roles it chooses to play or has chosen to play, or are they? I don't know.

Starting sometime in the thirties with a very cautious and careful reading of the New Deal mood of that time and the limits of government in this outlaw society of ours we set in motion the bandwagon that ultimately built more public, school, and college libraries than any other force in history, including Andrew Carnegie. The movement to convince our nation that there is a federal level responsibility to support libraries was a quiet, behind-the-scenes one at first. It didn't use a bandwagon until we really wanted to raid the U.S. Treasury. That movement illustrates something that happens with bandwagons. When you want a bigger parade you have to state your cause in a way that will attract varieties of people, people who often disagree with each other. Thus was first invented the great "unserved" population in America. We all know about the unserved, the nonuser. The feds could understand bringing library service to the "unserved" in rural communities. Then we talked about the need for buildings. The feds seemed to be able to understand that, and we even changed the name of the law from the Library Services Act to the Library Services and Construction Act. That got us a little more money. Rural libraries of course were always a part of that library cause.

School and college libraries got their own laws too. They got a big boost from the Soviet space program. You remember, it was the National Defense Education Act that built all those wonderful school library programs. Finally something called the systems concept was added along in that history somewhere whereby libraries would ban together in consortia to improve library service by sharing resources.

We used that federal money to build more buildings than ever before in the history of libraries. We used it to experiment with outreach programs, many of which survived the experimental phase and still work, many of which failed miserably but taught us a lot of lessons about it. Some of them lasted, like the job information centers in New York. We built those crazy multitype systems with that money—we'll see if they last. The best example of those are the ones in Illinois which Iron Duke Al Trezza forced upon the scene with the kind of leadership that you rarely see any more, good old Illinois political leadership.

So to sustain the bandwagon of federal support we changed the missions and the uses of the money, we wrote new slogans, and in truth built some great new services: some effective ones, some not so effective.

The social responsibility movement in librarianship had similar results and it kind of planned diffusion at its beginnings. That bandwagon really wanted a big parade — a great big parade. We were pretty mad. Anyone with any kind of cause was allowed to become a leader. It was the easiest thing in the world to go in there and start a SRRT (ALA's Social Responsibility Round Table) task force, and they gave you money!

Out of that movement grew ALA's Freedom to Read Foundation, the Feminist Task Force, the very prestigious ALA committee on the Status of Women. The Pay Equity committee came out of that movement. Librarians who served prisons were organized in the SRRT parade along with our Black Caucus, REFORMA (the Hispanic librarians), and our Gay and Lesbian Task Force.

The ALA governance freaks in the Social Responsibility parade accomplished really a great deal when you think about how difficult it is to accomplish things in organizations. All ALA meetings from the executive board to the lowliest committee, including all the meetings in the divisions, are now open to any member observer who wants to show up. A new level of democracy was achieved throughout the organization.

What started as a social responsibility bandwagon aimed at putting ALA on record in support of various social questions actually spawned a host of other parades, many of them making crucial contributions to our professional development as well as putting us on record behind some pretty good ideas.

One of my favorite bandwagon examples is the one called "information literacy." Now, I've been a public and academic reference librarian, and in both jobs I had that awful responsibility to show kids and adults how to use the damn library. As Tom Eadie pointed out in a *Library Journal* article (October 15, 1990), it never really worked. Library instruction was like a smallpox vaccination that didn't take. It occurs to me that here in the United States of America one of the very, very few nations that offers cradle to grave free libraries, there is really no earthly reason for a citizen not to know how to use a library. Yet we find it necessary, or we say it is necessary to mount expensive, time consuming remedial learning programs in the college libraries to teach people how to use the library. It's as if they had never been near one before at home or at school. Where were the librarians of our childhood?

Now Pat Breivik tells us we need to go beyond bibliographic instruction and give people something called "information literacy." I obviously need some of that therapy myself, because I don't even know what "information literacy" means. I'm sorry, I just couldn't bring myself to plow through that dense document they wrote on the subject. But I know it's there, I know there is one. We are in this crazy parade, but no one is beating the path to library doors to get some "information literacy."

I think this particular bandwagon effect is simply a reflection of the entrancement of some of us librarians with the elaborate and glorious apparatus — print and electronic apparatus — that we have all created to retrieve and manipulate information. We think it is so terrific that we want to show and tell to the rest of the population! I don't mind this, I'm very enthusiastic. I love Betty's enthusiasm for all this magic stuff. But what the rest of the population wants, alas, is not a lesson in how to use the apparatus or use libraries, they want the information! They will learn only what is necessary to get the information. Usually all they have to know is which librarian to ask, and I really don't see any big reason to change that. If electronic information systems are to succeed, in a society so trained in instant solutions, they will have to provide instant user friendliness (I should say instant information literacy). Now there's a fine bandwagon! It's like it is with instant coffee or frozen orange juice: the resulting drink doesn't have the authenticity, the natural flavor of the original, but it does deliver the caffeine or the vitamin C. We can market something like that — instant information! The information may be from a secondary source, or a little lacking in depth, but it will answer the question.

One thing Americans like is answers. We are not a process people. We would rather eat it than cook it. We would rather know it than learn it. Because librarians traditionally serve the crowd that does sometimes enjoy learning, they think that crowd represents popular America. The learning crowd is the top 2 percent or less. The rest want instant answers, not some highfalutin new kind of literacy. I don't cheer that news, you understand. I just feel as though we can't fight it with bibliographic instruction or information literacy programs.

Our best effort ought to be used to get answers to people quickly. So much for that parade. But do read Lawrence McCrank's very literate article debunking information literacy in the May 1, 1991 *LJ*. Even if you disagree with him, you will enjoy it.

John N. Berry III 55

Both the library hall of fame and the library junkyard are full of old bandwagons. With each generation, they get more elaborate. Why is that? Because it takes a better bandwagon to get experienced marchers to join yet another parade, and ours is an aging profession. Now that may explain why the recent bandwagons are a little less flamboyant and a little less ambitious.

Our bandwagons have actually served their purpose. In most instances they have brought both the appearance and the substance of change. They have left us with both physical and ideological monuments, shrines at which we regularly worship—ideas that shape our field. Despite that field's location, for the most part, in the public sector, it is low in corruption, high in service, it has an unequaled reservoir of public respect. Indeed libraries are among society's most cherished sacred cows. Ask any politician. Ask any college president. (I think there is a distinction in there, but I'm not sure.) Ask any business leader. Ask any of those guys and you'll get an instant how-I-was-educated-at-the-library speech.

At the substantive level, according to that Harris poll that I cited earlier, 65 percent of people over the age of eighteen use libraries on a regular basis and that is an amazing feat in a society hooked on instant gratification. I like to think that librarians were on a bandwagon that led our country to the most freedom of information and the most freedom of expression of any society yet known. I like to think that we had one glorious period where we convinced federal, state, and local governments that each has an identifiable responsibility to secure our right to know through free libraries.

We need new bandwagons to continue that work. Maybe our Japanese information gap or a national market share library act is the answer, I don't know. I would like to think that we created the perfect institution for a democracy like ours. It says that the information problem is a public problem, and requires a public solution. But, to cite other American bandwagons, "Don't tread on me. Leave me, the individual alone. Let me do damn near anything I choose to do. When I want information or reading, give it to me one-on-one. Serve me as an individual, not as a mass market. Let me seek information in as much or as little depth as I want."

We've created a communal institution that serves individual inquiry. Now that is a very worthy bandwagon to follow and to celebrate. Shall we have a parade?

Our best bandwagons—the ones that say that reading and libraries are good, books are good, and that all people have a right to know, a right to free information, are at the head of that citizen parade. Right now it leads more of our citizens than ever into libraries and we need those citizens for our next act — a bandwagon to convince voters and government that library support is crucial to our nation. I believe it is. I'm ready to march.

Discussion

Eddison: Ever since I became a librarian, I have been very puzzled why all our organizations and our publications talk about buildings – it's not the American Librarians Association; it's not the *Librarians Journal,* it's the *Library Journal;* it's not the Special Librarians Association, it's Special Libraries Association. Why? Do we have to hide behind brick? Why can't we be people?

Berry: Why not? I don't see anything wrong with that.

Eddison: It's part of the image problem. We're not standing up for ourselves. It's not our organizations that are joining together, it's we as individuals who are joining together.

Berry: I am more interested in the institution than any of the individuals that work in it. Like Charlie, I would like to see librarians get more money, and better status, but I'm not too concerned about the image. I never use the word "image." I am very upset about that study that SLA did which I think is one of the most condescending, demeaning pieces of work I've ever encountered on that subject. I think that our obsession with this image problem is a horrible error. I think that if you look at the people who use libraries, it might be a good idea to consider that we have an image that is very close to their image and I would let it go at that. I think that's the best way to look – like the people we serve. To be compatible and friendly and able to deal with them directly – we do that, and do it well. I am not one of those who thinks we have huge problems. We attract a lot of people, they like us, they vote – not enough money, but enough in support of the institution. If we want to have a librarians association, I'm for it, I would join. I would like to to take up issues like salaries and working conditions.

Robinson: How would you like to have a lawyer's image, or even a doctor's image?

Berry: Good point! I wouldn't.

Anne Mintz, Forbes: I would like to support Betty Eddison's point of view. When we talk about changes in an organization, in a school, for example, we don't talk about the school changing the community, we talk about the teacher who is the agent of change. Betty's point is that the librarian is the agent of change in a library. The library as an institution hasn't done anything in the community until the librarian has. When I was a student here twenty years ago, in the courses that dealt with public libraries, we were focusing on how to be agents of change in the communities we were going out into. We talked a lot about bookmobiles, we talked a lot about serving the needs of the people who were in that community — not the library but the librarian as agent. Betty's point is telling, and I don't think it's a specialist's point of view as opposed to public librarian's point of view. Just because I'm a special librarian doesn't mean that Betty and I are always going to agree on everything. I would like to see librarians be stronger agents of change and I would like to ask the panel for more recommendations. For example, how to create an environment for graduate students who can then go into jobs that will enable them to create change in their organizations?

Turock: I think that one thing that Betty has said is important and differs a great deal from what the usual management gurus have said. She talked about change as spontaneous and serendipitous, and those are things that are frequently missed when we look at the literature of management and they are very important. Anyone who has been involved as a change agent will recognize these and empathize with her when she says those words. There's a certain amount of seeing an opportunity that you believe will move something forward and seizing it.

Marc Eisen, East Orange Public Library: Even if we accept academic institutions as agents of change, possibly corporations as needing to change, public libraries differ greatly. There are some very changing communities; however, there are some very unchanging communities. In changing communities, would the panel care to comment on the public's need to perceive the library as a stable institution rather than as a changing institution. Sometimes the changes should not show to continue the feeling of stability of an institution of government.

Robinson: I think that one of the things that often we forget is how little control we have in public libraries, especially in some places. Let me give you an example. In the Free Library of Philadelphia, where Elliot Shelkrot is director — before him, Keith Doms, and before him, Emerson Greenaway — and in some other big city libraries, no matter what changes the director, or in some cases the director and the trustees, want to put in place, they have two very, very strong anti-change agents that will defeat them almost always: unions and the city government. It's gotten so that most of those libraries, because big government always wants more and more control, are not run by the library director. Any philosophy that she or he may have cannot be really implemented. The director is nothing but an accountant or kind of a caretaker for the city government. The city government makes all the decisions.

Pat O'Brien of Dallas was bewailing budget cuts at one ALA conference, and the last budget cuts that he came up with that week while he was getting telephone calls, was that he was to take a professional librarian out of each branch. And he said that even when they cut x number of dollars, they tell him where to cut it. Now my library is relatively free, it's legally free. We knew it was going to be a tight budget year next year, and we said OK, keeping the book budget the same or increasing the book budget is more important than being open on Sundays. The county came back and said we are going to give you the money to keep three libraries open on Sundays—we realize the book budget is your priority, but it's not ours. Who is running the library? The board? Or them? I think that one of the things that is not appreciated, not even by John in his editorial writing, is how little library directors can control things and how much the politicians do. Now, if the politicians are elected by the people, that is the people expressing themselves through their elected officials. In most cases where the people vote on the library budget, the library does well. Look at Long Island—they have $175 per capita, or some huge amount.

Berry: There's a great deal of truth in what you say about the political situation. Perhaps, in answer to the question about image, I will take back a part of what I said. If there is one glaring crisis in our ability to be change agents and to manage libraries, it is in that inability to manipulate the political process as well as others.

I take exception to the thing about education, because if there is any movement that is spreading like a brushfire, it is the movement to give our citizens control of the schools. They don't want any part of the teachers and they don't want any part of the educational administration any more and the government is aiding and abetting citizens in this cause. From the federal level on down, the people who get the hardest shots in politics in communities I observe are the teachers and the school administrators, who are accused of padding the budget. They've got state mandates that they want to repeal, and they have a library mandate here in New Jersey that they want to repeal, I realize.

My point is that we are not adept at manipulating the immense reservoir of political power we have and I think that if we did nothing else but a good crisis program to help us learn to do that—or just getting out there in the trenches—would be the most effective thing to do.

I spoke at a budget hearing in my community recently, because that public library is being savaged. This is a public library which is supported at $50 per capita, which is not bad. They cut this budget by a million bucks out of five million. That's 20 percent. I went down and testified, and was amazed by the reception. A dozen members of the board of finance and city council sought me out after the meeting. I spoke with as much passion as I could give to it and as much data as well. They said they were interested to hear what I had to say about the library—nobody had ever talked library to them, nobody had organized it!

There's a friends group there, there's a tremendous amount of support, but few went down to the meeting. There were fifty people there yelling about the school budget and ten cops who were arguing about police layoffs. I think we need to be better at that and I think that one way to do it is to enlist others. I don't think we have to do all that work always. I like the idea of municipal reference service. I have urged our library to get down to city hall and start peddling service to that crowd of politicians and officials. They are beginning to realize that it might be good to be in those offices with something those people could use.

Appendix A:
About Lowell Martin

Jana Varlejs

Rutgers was extraordinarily fortunate in choosing Lowell Martin to head its new Graduate School of Library Service in 1953. He recruited a stellar faculty, including Mary Gaver, Ralph Shaw, Keyes Metcalfe, and Margaret Monroe, and gained ALA accreditation of the MLS program within two years of its launching. He set the highest standards for the Rutgers GSLS, and earned the school a national reputation within a very short time.

Although Lowell Martin left Rutgers in 1959 to become Vice-President and Editorial Director of Grolier, Incorporated, his name is still linked with New Jersey. *Libraries for the People of New Jersey or Knowledge for All* (NJLA Library Development Committee, 1964), better known as the Martin-Gaver report, laid the foundation for regional library service in the state during the sixties and seventies, and remains a touchstone even today.

In addition to serving as dean at Rutgers, Lowell Martin has taught at the Chicago, Columbia, and SUNY Albany library schools. Early in his career, he worked in school, academic, and public libraries in Chicago. He obtained his master's and doctoral degrees from the Graduate Library School at the University of Chicago, where he completed a seminal thesis on "The Desirable Minimum Size of Public Library Units" (University of Chicago, 1945). It is to this research that we can trace, in part, the roots of regional cooperative library networks. He has also been instrumental in shaping our concept of what public library standards should be, advocating that prioritizing, planning, and evaluation at the local level should take precedence over national standards.

Lowell Martin is best known for his studies of large urban libraries, ranging from Philadelphia to San Francisco to Atlanta. The 1968–69 survey of the Chicago Public Library resulted in his book, *Library Response to Urban Change* (ALA, 1969), a model of thorough and creative analysis. Incidentally, Lowell Martin chose the research directors for this study from the Rutgers Ph.D. program: Terry Crowley and Tom Shaughnessy.

Lowell Martin could always be counted on to stimulate fresh thinking about library service, although his recommendations — frequently imaginative and sometimes controversial — were not always followed. Ultimately, however, he has succeeded in making a major impact on the thinking of the profession. For public librarianship, it virtually amounts to a paradigm shift. Best summarized in his 1982 Bowker Memorial Lecture, "The Public Library: Middle-age Crisis or Old Age?" his advice is to stop trying to be all things to all people, to identify each library's role in its community, and to "concentrate and strengthen" in the role area it selects. This advice has been taken to heart by the Public Library Association, and is reflected in its *Planning and Role Setting for Public Libraries* (ALA, 1987).

In 1979, Lowell Martin received the ALA's highest award, Honorary Life Membership. The citation read in part, "For a career marked by industry, eloquence, and integrity." To those characteristics, we would add innovation, leadership, and impact. It is with special pride that we confer upon him honorary membership in our alumni association, thereby giving long overdue recognition to the contributions made by Lowell Martin, the first dean of the Rutgers Graduate School of Library Service, to Rutgers, to New Jersey, and to the profession.

Appendix B:
Lowell A. Martin: A Biobibliography*

Mary Niles Maack

This biobibliography was begun as an effort to document, analyze and assess the remarkable contribution that Dr. Lowell Martin has made to the field of librarianship. Even though I have not yet completed the paper which will discuss in greater detail the ways that his research and his ideas have influenced the thinking and the practices of the profession, it seemed quite appropriate to include this listing of his published work in a volume honoring that contribution.

I first became acquainted with Professor Martin at Columbia School of Library Service where he had just resumed his teaching career after spending six years as Dean at Rutgers, followed by ten years at Grolier where he served as Editorial Director and Vice President. Then, in 1969, the year that ALA published his groundbreaking study of the Chicago Public Library (*Library Response to Urban Change*, Item #81), he returned to the classroom. As a student in his Urban Librarianship class I had the wonderful opportunity to share in the excitement surrounding the completion of this work which was hailed by reviewers as "revolutionary," (Bendix) "a stimulus to library planners" (Bloss) and "no less than a prescription, applicable in large measure, if not completely, to all urban library centers." (Carnovsky).

Dr. Martin's personal convictions about the role of the library in the community, which came across so vividly in the classroom, were eloquently expressed in the preface to that book:

> The very existence and vitality of the city are challenged; it
> has within it both the promise of greatness and the seeds of

Copyright © 1992 Mary Niles Maack.

destruction. A library does not stop riots or remove physical deterioration or eradicate prejudice. But an effective library, in its modest way, helps to get at the root causes of the urban problem: people unprepared to take their place in the economic order and people divided by lack of understanding. And an effective library serves to sustain the quality of life for all, not in utilitarian matters alone but also in the fulfillment of mind and spirit. (Item #81, p. xiii)

He goes on to say that "the urban condition calls for something more than 'business as usual.' " In the innovative plan that follows, he challenges the Chicago Public Library "to adjust to the people of the city in all their diversity, rather than expecting them to conform to a standardized institution." In the Chicago study, Dr. Martin presented all urban libraries with a challenge and a "call to excellence and innovation" (Item #81, p. xiii). Reading these words more than twenty years later—in Los Angeles, in the wake of one of the most tragic outbreaks of urban violence in our history—I am again struck by the timeliness of this ringing call to action.

My personal admiration for Lowell Martin's contribution to the creation of community based services grew tremendously when I was asked to teach a course on public libraries at the Graduate School of Library and Information Science at UCLA. As I prepared a selection of readings[1] which I hoped would introduce students to the intellectual and social foundations of the American public library, I felt compelled to draw heavily on Dr. Martin's work. His articles which were included in my first reader ranged from a seminal essay on "The American Public Library as a Social Institution" (published in *Library Quarterly* in 1937, Item #3) to the 1982 Bowker lecture (Item #99) and a 1984 article dealing with "Urban Libraries in the Sunbelt" (Item #102). In this span of nearly fifty years, the theme that emerged like a leitmotif was the continuing emphasis on libraries focused clearly on the needs of the people—both traditional users and potential users.

His conviction that community meant the *whole* community—including the underserved and those who lacked the skills and knowledge to use traditional library services—was apparent in his early work. In 1944 in a paper on "Community Analysis for the Library" (Item #9) Martin stressed the use of this kind of research to extend the service of the library beyond the self-selected few who were already regular users. He writes:

A community survey is a means for overcoming the narrow social base on which much public library service rests. Librar-

ians justify many books and services in terms of "demand."
... It is a questionable basis however when demand is taken as the request of the minority who happen to be attracted to present library offerings. ... Community analysis identifies the total community picture as against that part of the picture which can be seen from the library's information desk. (Item #9, p. 203).

Five years later when he was invited to discuss the Berelson report from the Public Library Inquiry, Martin's remarks were diplomatic; he praised many of the study's conclusions and did not openly challenge Berelson's view that libraries should serve their traditional clientele, but serve them better. Nonetheless at the Forum on the Public Library Inquiry, Martin asserted that "the future of the library depends upon ascertaining the needs of the people that are not met by the expanding communications networks and in concentrating our energies upon them." (Item #22, p. 49). Over three decades later, he was to use "concentrate and strengthen" as a theme for his Bowker lecture at Columbia, and once again he maintained the importance of serving the needs of the people. He writes: "Each library and community . . . must decide what they want to accomplish and then mobilize resources to that end." (Item #99, p. 21). Two years later, when reflecting on libraries in the West, he urged librarians "to go outside the four walls,to identify and empathize with our users, present and potential, . . . to seek to understand people as individuals, people searching for self-realization." (Item #102, p. 84).

Martin's research in cities such as Chicago and Baltimore clearly showed the distance between the ideal of serving everyone and the reality of the library as an institution that too often turned inward on itself. Nonetheless, his recommendations were often grounded in the belief that libraries had a responsibility "to be sure that full opportunity is kept open for a person born and brought up in a setting that stifles his potentialities." (Item #71, p. 39). The ongoing tension between beliefs and actions, between constraints and opportunities, between potential service and present practice also were made evident to his students.

Professor Martin inspired us by his dedication, breadth of knowledge and rigorous approach to research. However, because he believed that learning must also be linked to experience, he divided us into teams and sent us into the community. Our assignment was to talk with residents, librarians, friends of the library, non-users, local leaders, workers, children, teachers, and other professionals. Our task was to find out about their need for information as well as their perceptions of the local library. This experirence left an indelible impression, enabling us to understand a bit more about the reality of bureaucratic institutions as well as developing in us a commitment to reach out beyond the comfortable confines of the library. Through his research, his experience and his creative approach to teaching Professor Martin influenced countless students who have used many of his ideas to improve, extend and adapt library services to meet the needs of their communities.

As I reflected back on Lowell Martin's accomplishments as a teacher, it seemed that his work embodied scholarship in all its many dimensions. As Ernest Boyer from the Carnegie Foundation defined the work of the professoriate, it should include: "the scholarship of *discovery,* the scholarship of *integration;* the scholarship of *application;* and the scholarship of *teaching.*"[2] Lowell Martin has contributed original research—the scholarship of discovery—through the many studies he carried out in public libraries over a span of nearly four decades. He not only did careful studies for major city libraries such as Enoch Pratt in Baltimore, the Chicago Public Library, and the Atlanta Public Library, but he also worked on the development of statewide planning from New Jersey and Pennsylvania to California. Although his advice as a consultant was not always implemented by the libraries he studied, his published work integrated these findings into a new conceptual framework based on a user-centered approach to library services. By pushing the profession in new directions, these ideas and findings had an impact that went far beyond the individual states or cities that had commissioned his work. An early advocate of moving from quantitative standards to community needs assessment, Dr. Martin's published speeches and articles as well as his research clearly influenced the profession to adopt the planning process in place of the old standards.

The biobibliography of Lowell Martin's work that follows is restricted to those published books, articles, and book reviews that were indexed in H. W. Wilson's *Library Literature.*[3] Although Dr. Martin authored other reports which were not formally published by those who commissioned his work, these items are not easily accessible and were therefore not included.

The bibliography is divided into three sections: Part I includes original works, Part II is limited to book reviews by Dr. Martin and Part III contains a listing of biographical sketches and announcements. Each part is arranged chronologically and all entries in Part I and Part II are numbered consecutively. In Part I monographs are separated from articles in order to give prominence to these more lengthy studies. The listing of reviews that follows these books, monographs or reports are a part of the entry for the work itself and have not been numbered.

References

1. Mary Niles Maack, *Readings on Public Libraries* (Los Angeles: UCLA Academic Publishing Services, 1987).
2. Ernest L. Boyer, *Scholarship Reconsidered: Priorities of the Professoriate* (Princeton, NJ: The Carnegie Foundation for the Advancement of Teaching, 1990) 16.
3. I would like to acknowledge the work of David Johnson, who did much of the searching, photocopied articles, and input most of the citations while he was employed as my research assistant at UCLA.

PART I. Original Works

1935   **Article**

1. "What is this library science?" *Library Journal* 60:974-75 (December 15, 1935).

1936   **Article**

2. "High school library." *Library Journal* 61:840-42 (November 1, 1936).

1937   **Article**

3. "American public library as a social institution." *Library Quarterly* 7:546-63 (October 1937). [Reprinted in] *American library philosophy: an anthology.* Hamden, CT: Shoe String Press, 1975. p. 88-105.

1939   **Article**

4. "Public library provision of books about social problems." *Library Quarterly* 9:249-72 (July 1939).

1940   **Thesis (M.A.)**

5. Purpose and administrative organization of branch systems in large urban libraries. 109p. University of Chicago.

1941   **Monographs and Reports**

6. [with Miles, Arnold] *Public administration and the library.* (University of

Chicago studies in library science). Chicago: University of Chicago Press [1941].

Reviews

Ferguson, M. J. *Library Journal* 66:1084 (December 15, 1941).
Beals, R. A. *College & Research Libraries* 3:262-63 (June 1942).
Vitz, C. *Library Quarterly* 12:858-61 (October 1942).
Cashmore, H. M. *Library Review* No. 69:147 (Spring 1944).

Article

7. "Chicago's experimental library" *Illinois Libraries* 23:23 (June 1941).

1942   Article

8. "Second things second; the library after the war. *Library Occurrent* 14:83-8 (October/December 1942).

1944   Monographs, Reports and Chapters

9. [edited with Carnovsky, Leon] *Library in the community; papers presented before the Library Institute at the University of Chicago, August 23-28, 1943.* University of Chicago Press, 1944.

Reviews

Butler, H. L. *Catholic Library World* 16:60 (November 1944).
Foster, J. H. *Library Quarterly* 15:78-9 (January 1945).
Roden, C. B. *Library Journal* 70:115-16 (February 1, 1945).
Canadian Library Council Bulletin 1:60-1 (June 1945).

10. "Community analysis for the library" In *Library in the community.* p. 201-14.

1945   Monographs, Reports and Chapters

11. "Optimum size of the public library unit." In Joeckel, C. B. (ed.) *Library extension, problems and solutions; papers presented before the Library Institute at the University of Chicago, August 21-26, 1944,* Chicago: University of Chicago Press, 1945, p. 32-46.

Thesis (Ph.D.)

12. Desirable minimum size of public library units. University of Chicago.

Article

13. "Shall library schools teach administration?" *College & Research Libraries* 6:335-40+ (September 1945).

1946   Monographs, Reports and Chapters

14. [edited] *Personnel administration in libraries; papers presented before the*

Library Institute at the University of Chicago, August 27–September 1, 1945. Chicago: University of Chicago Press, 1946.

Reviews

Shaw, R. R. *Library Journal* 71:1458–59 (October 15, 1946).
Rice, P. N. *Library Quarterly* 17:62 (January 1947).
United States Quarterly Book List 3:79–80 (March 1947).

15. "Toward a qualified postwar library personnel." In *Personnel administration in libraries.* p. 148–60.

Articles

16. "Guided group reading as a library service; the Chicago project." *Library Journal* 71:734–39 (May 15, 1946).

17. "National plan for public library service." *ALA Bulletin* 40:276–83 (September 1946).

1947   Article

18. "Direction of professional education for librarianship." *Minnesota Libraries* 15:207–09 (September 1947).

1948   Monographs, Reports and Chapters

19. "Potential role of the American public library." In American Library Association. Post-war Planning Committee. *National plan for public library service.* p. 1–17. American Library Association, 1948.

Article

20. "Potential role of the American public library." [Revised version]. *Public Libraries* 2:63–65 (December 1948).

1950   Monographs, Reports and Chapters

21. "What conclusions follow from the changing concepts of adequacy in terms of program and support in reference to the basic costs of library service?" In New York Library Association. [Conference, 56th, 1949, Syracuse] *Pre-conference: Legislative program in the light of recent developments.* 1950.

22. "The Library's Public by Bernard Berelson: Discussion by Lowell Martin, Associate Dean, School of Library Service, Columbia University." In Asheim, Lester E., ed. *A Forum on the Public Library Inquiry.* New York: Columbia University Press, 1950.

1952   Articles

23. "Public librarian." *Public Libraries* 6:7–9 (April 1952).

24. "Impressions of Missouri libraries." *MLA Quarterly* 13:97–104 (December 1952).

1954   Article

25. "Training school librarians at Rutgers." *New Jersey School Librarian* 10:5 (Fall 1954).

1955   Monographs, Reports and Chapters

26. "Implications for the education of librarians." In Asheim, Lester E., ed. *Future of the Book.* p. 83–95.

Articles

27. "Library service to adults." *Library Quarterly* 25:1–14 (January 1955).

28. "Briefs of testimony: program progress." *Library Journal* 80:719–23 (April 1, 1955).

29. "Progress on new public library standards." *Public Libraries* 9:32–33 (May 1955).

30. "Progress on new public library standards." *ALA Bulletin* 49:296–97 (June 1955).

31. "Implications for the education of librarians." *Library Quarterly* 25: 363–75 (October 1955).

1956   Articles

32. "How good is your library?" *Saturday Review of Literature* 39:13–15 (June 16, 1956).

33. "Public library service to America." *Maine Library Association Bulletin* 17:3–4 (August 1956).

1957   Monographs and Reports

34. *Library service for Baltimore county: a report to the County Librarian and Board of Library Trustees.* Baltimore, MD: Baltimore County Library. 202p. 1957.

Reviews

Hamill, H. L. *Library Journal* 84:407 (February 1, 1959).
Moehlenbrock, S. *Biblioteksbladet* 44(7):521–2 (1959).

Articles

35. "New goals for library service." *Vermont Bulletin* 52:66–71 (March 1957).

36. "New goals for library service." *South Dakota Library Bulletin* 43:34–38 (April/June 1957).

37. "Research in education for librarianship." *Library Trends* 6:207–18 (October 1957).

38. Library standards and the federal program." *Library Journal* 82:2315-17 (October 1, 1957).

39. "New national standards for public libraries." *Wisconsin Library Bulletin* 53:523-28 + (November 1957).

40. "Work-study programs—recruiting breakthrough?" *Library Journal* 82: 2743-49 (November 1, 1957).

1958   **Monographs and Reports**

41. *Branch library service for Dallas: a report sponsored by the Friends of the Dallas Public Library.* Dallas, TX: Friends of the Dallas Public Library, 1958.

Review

Geddes, A. *Library Journal* 83:830 (March 15, 1958).

42. Library service in Pennsylvania, present and proposed: a survey. 2 vols. Harrisburg, PA: Pennsylvania State Library, 1958.

Review

Munn, R. *Library Quarterly* 29:267-68 (October 1959).

43. *Summary of recommendations of the Pennsylvania library survey: a study of library service in Pennsylvania with a proposal for a state-wide plan of public library development, with assistance of an advisory committee appointed by the Pennsylvania Library Association.* Harrisburg, PA: Pennsylvania State Library, 1958.

Articles

44. "Do the standards come up to standard?" *ALA Bulletin* 52:755-60 (November 1958).

45. "Pennsylvania library survey—a progress report." *Pennsylvania Library Association Bulletin* 13:21 (Winter 1958).

1959

46. "Relation of public and school libraries in serving youth." *ALA Bulletin* 53:112-17 (February 1959).

47. "Relation of public and school libraries in serving youth." *National Association of Secondary-School Principals Bulletin* 43:173-77 (November 1959). [condensed version]

48. "County and regional libraries: hope and reality." *Minnesota Libraries* 19:147-54 (June 1959).

1960   **Articles**

49. "Establishing standards for libraries." *Canadian Library Association Bulletin* 16:224-27 (March 1960).

50. "Establishing standards for libraries." *Canadian Library Association Feliciter* 8:11-14 (March 1963).

51. "Library interdependence and joint action." *MLA Quarterly* 21:24-35 (March 1960).

52. "State-wide library planning." *Florida Libraries* 11:3-4 (June 1960).

53. "Blueprint for public libraries in India." *Library Journal* 85:2110-13 (June 1, 1960).

1962   **Monographs, Reports and Chapters**

54. "LSA and library standards: two sides of the coin." In University of Illinois. Graduate School of Library Science. *Impact of the Library Services Act: progress and potential.* p. 1-16. Champaign, IL: Illini Union Bookstore, 1962.

Articles

55. "Deiches studies of Pratt Library examine student reading." *Maryland Libraries* 29:2-11 (Fall 1962).

56. [and Castagna, Edwin] "Deiches studies of the Enoch Pratt free library." *Maryland Libraries* 28:15-16 (Winter 1962).

57. "Look ahead, state-wide library planning." *Ohio Library Association Bulletin* 32:3-7 (October 1962).

1963   **Monographs and Reports**

58. *Students and the Pratt Library: challenge and opportunity.* (Deiches fund studies of public library service, No. 1.) Baltimore, MD: Enoch Pratt Free Library, 1963. 68p.

Review

Carnovsky, L. *Library Quarterly* 34:132-3 (January 1964).

Article

59. "Conference-within-a-conference: Lowell Martin's CWC summary." *ALA Bulletin* 57:734-41 (September 1963).

1964   **Monographs, Reports and Chapters**

60. [and Gaver, M. V.] *Libraries for the people of New Jersey: or, Knowledge for all.* New Brunswick, NJ: New Jersey Library Association. Development Committee, 1964. 83p.

61. "Summary of the group recommendations." In American Library Association. *Student Use of Libraries.* p. 189-99. Chicago: American Library Association, 1964.

Articles

62. "Timetable for action: a summary and critique." *News Notes of California Libraries* 59:391-398 (Summer 1964) [portrait of the author, p. 346]

63. "Library Services and Construction Act, what will it mean?" *ALA Bulletin* 58:689-94 (September 1964).

64. "Patterns of partnership." *Library Journal* 89:4593-96 (November 15, 1964).

65. "Patterns of partnership." *School Library Journal* 11:19-22 (November 1964). [same]

1965   Monographs and Reports

66. [and Bowler, Roberta] *Public library service equal to the challenge of California: a report to the state librarian.* Sacramento, CA: California State Library, 1965. 132p.

Reviews

Reilly, A. F. *California Librarian* 27:47-50 (January 1966).
Blasingame, Jr., R. *Library Journal* 91:2808-09 (June 1, 1966).
Connor, J. L. *News Notes of California Libraries* 61:217-21 (Spring 1966).
Hauge, M. *Reol* No. 4:250-51 (1966).

67. [as Consultant.] Boaz, Martha T. *Strength through cooperation in Southern California libraries: a survey.* Los Angeles: n.p., 1965. 175p.

Articles

68. "Can our good encyclopedias be made better?" *RQ* 5:6-9 (Winter 1965).

69. "State and federal aid for libraries in New Jersey." *New Jersey Libraries:* 7 (March 1965).

70. "Ski resorts and glass branches." *Library Journal* 90:2076-77 (May 1, 1965).

1967   Monographs, Reports and Chapters

71. *Baltimore reaches out: library services to the disadvantaged.* (Deiches fund studies of public library services. No. 3.) Baltimore, MD: Enoch Pratt Free Library, 1967. 54p.

Reviews

Moon, E. E. *Library Journal* 92:3617-18 (October 15, 1967).
Bloss, M. *Library Quarterly* 38:122-24 (January 1968).
Ashmore, W. S. H. *Library Association Record* 70:221-22 (August 1968).
Glistrup, J. B. *Scandinavian Public Library Quarterly* 3(1):48-49 (1970).

72. "Library in the city." [reprinted from *Baltimore reaches out.*] In Reynolds,

Michael M. and Daniels, Evelyn H., eds. *Reader in library and information services,* p. 117-21. Englewood, CO: Microcard Edition Books, 1974.

73. *Progress and problems of Pennsylvania libraries: a re-survey.* (Pennsylvania State Library Monograph, No. 6) Harrisburg, PA: Pennsylvania State Library, 1967. 59p.

Review

Hoy, E. M. *Ontario Library Review* 52:169-70 (September 1968).

74. "Personnel in library surveys." In Tauber, M. F. and Stephens, I. R., eds. *Library Surveys.* p. 123-41. New York: Columbia University Press, 1967.

Articles

75. "Libraries: the light at the end of the tunnel." *Arizona Librarian* 24:15-16+ (Spring 1967).

76. "Re-survey of public libraries in Pennsylvania." *Pennsylvania Library Association Bulletin* 22:181-85 (May 1967).

1968   **Articles**

77. "Changes ahead [for libraries and publishing]." *Library Journal* 93:711-16 (February 15, 1968).

78. "Changing perspectives in librarianship." *Illinois Libraries* 50:195-205 (March 1968).

79. "Changing perspectives in librarianship." *Virginia Librarian* 15:14-24 (Summer 1968).

1969   **Monographs, Reports and Chapters**

80. "Emerging trends in interlibrary cooperation." In University of Illinois, Urbana. Graduate School of Library Science. *Cooperation between types of libraries: the beginnings of a state plan for library services in Illinois.* p. 1-11. Urbana, IL: Illini, 1969.

81. *Library response to urban change: a study of the Chicago public library.* Chicago: American Library Association, 1969. 313p.

Reviews

Campbell, H. C. *Library Association Record* 72:105-06 (March 1970).
Mallon, N. F. *Canadian Library Journal* 27:140-41 (March 1970).
Carnovsky, L. *Library Quarterly* 40:269-70 (April 1970).
Castagna, E. *College & Research Libraries* 31:203-4 (May 1970).
Maidment, W. R. *Journal of Documentation* 26:166-67 (June 1970).
Bebbington, J. *Library Review* 22:314-15 (Summer 1970).
Bendix, D. and L. Katz. *Drexel Library Quarterly* 6:346-9 (July/October 1970).

Ellsworth, R. C. *Ontario Library Review* 54:173-75 (September 1970).

Bloss, M. *Journal of Library History* 5:375-79 (October 1970).

Gurbielowa, M. *Bibliotekarz* 40(9):284-87 (1973).

82. "Library trustee and ALA standards." In Young, V. G. ed. *Library Trustee: a practical guidebook*. p. 102-09. New York: Bowker, 1969.

Articles

83. "What next in library services." *Tennessee Librarian* 21:49-53 (Winter 1969).

84. "Our own modest genius." *Wilson Library Bulletin* 43:851-53 (May 1969).

1970   Monographs, Reports and Chapters

85. "Suburban system in metropolitan library networks" [with discussion]. In North Suburban Library System, Morton Grove, IL, *Proceedings of NSLS Day 1969*, p. 3-20. Lowell Martin, 1970.

Article

86. "Suburban system in metropolitan library networks." *Illinois Libraries* 53:197-213 (March 1971).

1971   Article

87. "Library perspectives in the 1970s." *Minnesota Libraries* 23:158-63 (Summer 1971).

1972   Monographs, Reports and Chapters

88. "Role and structure of metropolitan libraries." In Conant, Ralph W. and Molz, Kathleen, eds. *Metropolitan Library*. p. 171-86. Cambridge, MA: MIT Press, 1972.

Articles

89. "Future of the urban main library." *Library Trends* 20:774-87 (April 1972).

90. "Standards for public libraries." *Library Trends* 21:164-77 (October 1972).

1973   Monographs, Reports and Chapters

91. "Philadelphia project: the Action Library, its purpose and program." In Garrison, Guy, ed. Conference on total community library service, 1972, Washington, D.C. *Total community library service*. p. 129-35. Chicago: American Library Association, 1973.

1974   Article

92. [Reply to Sarah R. Reed] *Library Trends* 22:403-13 (January 1974).

1976   **Article**

93. "User studies and library planning." *Library Trends* 24:483–96 (January 1976).

1979   **Monographs, Reports and Chapters**

94. "Future of the urban main library." In *Future of the main urban library.* p. 27–54. Urban Libraries Council, 1979.

95. [Comments.] In *Future of the main urban library.* p. 55–59.

Article

96. "Demographic trends and social structure." *Library Trends* 27:269–98 (Winter 1979).

1981   **Monographs, Reports and Chapters**

97. "Late great public library—R.I.P." In American Library Association. *ALA Yearbook, 1981.* p. 1–5. Chicago: American Library Association, 1981.

Article

98. "Library planning and library standards: historical perspectives." *Bookmark* 39:253–60 (Summer 1981).

1983   **Monographs, Reports and Chapters**

99. *Public library: middle-age crisis or old age?"* Tenth of the R. R. Bowker memorial lectures, new series, November 16, 1982. New York: Bowker, 1983. 29p.

Review

Stevens, N. D. *Wilson Library Bulletin* 58:62–63 (September 1983).

Commentary

[Discussion.] *Library Journal* 108:852 (May 1, 1983).
[Discussion.] *Library Journal* 108:932 (May 15, 1983).

Article

100. "Public Library: middle-age crisis or old age?" *Library Journal* 108:17–22 (January 1, 1983).

1984   **Monographs and Reports**

101. *Organizational structure of libraries.* (Library administration series No. 5.) Metuchen, NJ: Scarecrow Press, 1984. 294p.

Reviews

Stevens, N. D. *Wilson Library Bulletin* 59:284–85 (December 1984).

Sullivan, P. *Library Journal* 110:126 (February 15, 1985).
Mott, W. R. *Journal of Academic Librarianship* 11:100 (May 1985).
Hildesheim, P. M. A. *Canadian Library Journal* 42:227-28 (August 1985).
Webster, D. E. *College & Research Libraries* 46:443-44 (September 1985).
Edwards, R. M. *Public Library Quarterly* 7:81-82 (Spring/Summer 1986).
Library Review 35:130-31 (Summer 1986).

1986   Article

102. "Urban libraries in the sunbelt: views on public library service." *Public Libraries* 25:79-84 (Fall 1986).

PART II. *Reviews by Lowell Martin*

103. *High school science library for 1936-37.* In *Library Quarterly* 8:311-12 (April 1938).

104. *Administration of the American public library* by McDiarmid, E. W. Chicago: American Library Association & University of Illinois Press, 1943. In *Library Quarterly* 14:247-49 (July 1944).

105. *Report of a survey of the Charlotte Public Library to the board of trustees of the Charlotte Public Library* by Lowe, John A. Chicago: American Library Association, 1944. In *Library Quarterly* 16:76-78 (January 1946).

106. *Toward improving Ph.D. programs* by Hollis, Ernest V. Washington, D.C.: American Council on Education, 1945. In *College & Research Libraries* 7:188-89 (April 1946).

107. *Foundations of library management.* In *Library Quarterly* 19:289-90 (October 1949).

108. *Core of education for librarianship* by Asheim, L. ed. University of Chicago Graduate Library School. Chicago: American Library Association, 1954. In *Library Quarterly* 24:268-69 (July 1954).

PART III. *Biographical Sketches and Articles*

1946

Library Journal 71:1342 (October 1, 1946).

1947

"Becomes associate dean." *Library Journal* 72:333 (February 15, 1947).
College & Research Libraries 8:182-83 (April 1947).

1952

Special Libraries 43:181 (May–June 1952).

1953

Library Journal 78:1214 (July 1953).
Library Journal 78:1834 (October 15, 1953).

1955

Library Quarterly 25:128 (January 1955).

1962

"New honorary member, Dr. Lowell A. Martin." *New Jersey Library Association Newsletter* p. 20. (September 1962).

1964

"Lowell A. Martin, vice president and editorial director of Grolier, Inc." *Ohio Library Association Bulletin* 32:24 (October 1964).

1965

"Appointment of Lowell A. Martin to do a general study of state plans." *ALA Bulletin* 59:699 (September 1965).

1968

"Lowell A. Martin appointed professor of library service at Columbia University's School of Library Service." *NYLA Bulletin* 16:186 (November 1968).
"Lowell A. Martin appointed professor of library service at Columbia University's School of Library Service." *Wilson Library Bulletin* 43:314 (December 1968).

1970

"1970 ALA awards winner: Scarecrow Press award for library literature." *American Libraries* 1:813 (September 1970).
[same] *Library of Congress Information Bulletin* 29:A128 (September 3, 1970).
[same] *Wilson Library Bulletin* 45:33 (September 1970).

1979

"Honorary life member [of ALA]." *American Libraries* 10:381 (June 1979).
Also in: *Library Journal* 104:1524 (August 1979).
Also in: *Wilson Library Bulletin* 54:26 (September 1979).

1980

[portrait] In American Library Association. *ALA Yearbook, 1980.* Chicago: American Library Association, 1980. p. 77.

1983

"Lowell Martin's Atlanta PL study bares flaws, prescribes remedies." *Library Journal* 108:1074+ (June 1, 1983).

Commentary

[Discussion.] *Library Journal* 109:4 (January 1984).
Broderick, D. M. ed. Whose job is it anyway?" *Voice of Youth Advocates* 6(6):320–26 (February 1984).

1984

"Lowell Martin in Memphis." *Library Journal* 109:1172 (June 15, 1984).

About the Contributors

John N. Berry III has been editor-in-chief of *Library Journal* since 1969. He worked in the Reading (MA) Public Library while earning his MLS from Simmons College. He was a lecturer at the Simmons library school and assistant director of the College's library prior to joining the R. R. Bowker Company as assistant editor of *Library Journal* in 1964.

Elizabeth Bole Eddison, another Simmons MLS, is vice president and board chair of Inmagic, Inc. in Cambridge, Massachusetts. With Alice Warner, she founded the consulting firm of Warner-Eddison Associates in 1973. She serves on the Massachusetts Board of Library Commissioners and is on the board of the Special Libraries Association. She has received a number of honors, of which the most recent is the Information Industry Association's Entrepreneur Award.

Mary Jo Lynch has served as executive director of the American Library Association's Office for Research since 1978. She has been instrumental in the development and publication of the Public Library Association's planning process and output measures manuals, and in the nation-wide coordination of the collection of statistical data on public libraries. Her Ph.D. is from Rutgers.

Mary Niles Maack is associate dean and associate professor at the Graduate School of Library and Information Science at the University of California, Los Angeles. She earned her DLS from Columbia in 1978, and has served on the faculties of the University of Southern Illinois and the University of Minnesota. The American Library Association's Library History Round Table has honored her with the Justin Winsor Award.

Charles W. Robinson, yet another Simmons MLS graduate, directs the Baltimore County Public Library. He has served on many American Library Association bodies, including Council, and has been president of the Public Library Association. He has been involved in the PLA's projects on planning and output measures, as well as the *Cost-Finding Manual*.

Betty J. Turock chairs the Library and Information Studies Department and directs the MLS program at Rutgers, where she earned her MLS and Ph.D. degrees. The author of over sixty publications centering on public libraries, she is the founding editor of *Bottom Line*. Her most recent publications deal with the assessment of federally funded library programs for the U.S. Department of Education. She currently serves on the American Library Association's Executive Board.

Jana Varlejs is director of Professional Development Studies and associate professor at Rutgers SCILS. She has edited the annual symposium proceedings since 1982.